IF YOU COULD CHOOSE FROM MY CUP

Copyright © 2019. No part of this publication may be reproduced, stored in a retrieval system, or transmitted in any form or by any means, electronic, photocopying, mechanical or otherwise, without the prior written permission of the publishers.

ISBN 978-0-9958075-1-8

CIP info is available on request.

Printed in Canada by The Aylmer Express

Tracey can be contacted at: innerspacejourney@gmail.com.

Dedication

*I would like to dedicate the pages of this book
to all the amazing souls to whom I am connected.*

*Without your mentorship, trust, support, love,
and openness to share your experiences,
I would not have come to understand the meaning
or the passion I have for sharing my own eternal cup.*

Always with gratitude.
Love and light be yours.

Tracey L. Pagana

Acknowledgements

I would like, first and foremost, to thank The Divine for all the lessons and all that keeps us connected, flowing in and out of my life.

I am grateful for the stability of my life partner, Joe, who has taught me the deepest form of intimacy and respect throughout our relationship. Joe encourages growth even when I want to resist it.

I am eternally grateful for my incredibly talented editor, who spins my words into golden threads, weaving the chapters into something we call "medicine" in the hopes they may heal our readers. Susan Talbot, it is like you crawl right inside my heart and soul, helping me to get out the messages that are inside me so they are understandable and magical on paper.

For the beautiful gift of art: the cover holds a special healing white magic all of its own. Tanya Griffin, thank you for the hours you poured over this creation, honing the message of what's inside the cover, bringing that message to life. In simple, subliminal complexity, it unfolds before our eyes.

To Jodi Lennox, who provided the Foreword for this book: Thank you for your beautiful, kind words, for sharing your story, and for your bravery in choosing to share your thoughts so soon after losing your beautiful Mother.

For everyone who poured their hearts into the chapters of this book, sharing your personal journeys: Your honesty, truths, beliefs, lessons, and writing captivated me and taught me through the gift of sharing your journey with others. Dr. Wayne Dyer, Tanya Griffin, Natasha Ohler, Cate O'Neil, Maria Webb, Laurie Smydo, and Keegan Lesic: I will, now and forever, be grateful for and humbled by your courage and deep awareness, knowing that you needed to say what you did, but even more, that the world needed to hear it.

A huge 'Thank You' to all whose stories are shared in this book, but whose names are not revealed. With your permission, our connections and stories have been shared, along with the lessons they continue to bring us as we converse, unite, and heal ourselves.

Love and light.
Forever yours,

Tracey L. Pagana

Foreword
by Jodi Lennox

"I felt her before I saw her."

Those were my mom's first words after meeting Tracey for the first time.

My mom wasn't a big believer in the spiritual world. I was a believer, but was very unsure of its place in my life and pretty closed off about exploring further. That is, until I got to know Tracey.

My mom was diagnosed with Stage IV Pancreatic Cancer at age 67, in July 2017. Her diagnosis turned our world upside down. We were lost and scared. I personally suffered from significant anxiety. The future was so uncertain. It was like there were a million puzzle pieces, none of which were fitting together. Between doctors' visits and her first chemotherapy, we went to our summer vacation home for some family time. My mom wasn't feeling well, but was stoic for us. Tracey, who is a friend of my husband's family, happened to be in the area and had agreed to meet with my mom.

What followed after that first meeting can only be described as a gift from The Divine. My mom, Tracey, and I ended up being so intertwined, and she ended up filling our journey with an indescribable amount of love and peace. Tracey truly felt my mom from near or far. She could sense when mom was struggling, which would often be when she was alone at night. My mom would tell me the next day that she could actually feel Tracey's presence and light when she was feeling the most alone, and that it helped her through her darkest hours. Tracey gave her a sense of peace and contentment. I believe with all of my heart that Tracey helped my mom heal from past life trauma and helped her to prepare to transition to Heaven.

And once it was time to transition, our God-given connection to Tracey only grew. Tracey was there in spirit and in countless phone calls through the entire process, helping my mom pass over to Heaven on her own terms and with peace and dignity. It was like she was sitting in the room with us, because that's how strong and special her spirit is. One night, she sang Amazing Grace to us over the phone, over and over, and it was like an angel was there to comfort us and help us let go.

Through this process, my interconnection with Tracey grew even stronger. She could feel my turmoil, my struggle, and precociously gave me loving affirmation. I regularly heard from Tracey at 12:29 a.m. or p.m., which happens to be my mom's birthday. When my mom took her last breath, Tracey felt it: 2:57 a.m. I was sound asleep and heard her voice gently tell me my mom had passed. When I received the call at 4:30 a.m. that she was gone, I already knew and was at peace as my angel had already let me know. I get chills to this day thinking about it and feel so blessed and fortunate to have her in my life.

A few days later, Tracey told me that she was receiving a message for me to look up the meaning of angel number 313. I didn't ask why; I just looked it up. Not long into the future, I was searching for a home for my mom's beloved, deaf pit bull (not an easy home to find). The potential new owner's best friend was there, and we were talking about our mothers. She said her mother died at 3:13 and everywhere she goes she sees the number 313. I knew, without a doubt, that I had found the perfect home for my mom's dog.

Through all of this, I have found my ability to see the signs being sent to me from Heaven and to connect to the angelic realm. Channeling Tracey's love, energy and light has given me the power to discover my own internal healer. I have made myself stronger and happier, and by doing this, my internal cup is fuller and the puzzle pieces that were not fitting together seem to be falling into place. I have chosen to drink from Tracey's cup, and I can only encourage each reader to choose from her cup, as well. Open your hearts to love and the abilities that lie within you to heal yourself, and seize the opportunities that the universe presents to you when you least expect it.

Tracey was put on earth to help others, and the full breadth of her healing and spiritual gifts, I believe, has yet to be discovered.

Introduction

This book's inspiration and the courage to write it came to manifest when I received a referral who contacted me for a session. To say that our conversation and healing were not totally anointed from the very few first sentences out of our mouths would totally be an understatement. She was searching; she truly was committed to something she started to remember during her session; she further bravely committed to waking up. She is a powerful healer in her own right and is remembering all the truth that comes with those gifts. She filled my cup by telling me she sees me sending blessings everywhere and setting examples of kindness, like a shower raining love. She says I have accepted my resonance with spirit in such a commonsensical matter. What a compliment! Such appreciation of my spirit and my life! How could that not fill my cup to overflowing? This gave me the idea to write this book and I hope that it inspires others to keep their cups fully open, exposing their own magnificence and allowing the natural flow of self-healing love.

If you would like to know how I continue to fill my cup, I invite you all to read on with me. I would like to offer you overflowing abundance of love in the form of sharing with you my lessons of experience, tools, and methods that worked to help me grow and heal. These lessons fill me to the brim daily through their rich experience in many forms; tools and teachers sharing a combination of vast knowledge connected to and from The Divine and interacting with and for each other.

All the chapters that follow are based on personal experiences: joy, pain, sorrow. These treasures and lessons of knowledge have been a prerequisite to keeping my overflowing cup full of promise, supporting eternal new life. There is an ingredient to this way of living: that is, to share everything with everyone. This includes all and leaves no one out of this invitation. You will also read chapters on many different forms of healing methods. I have invited other healers to enlighten you and others by telling their courageous stories of finding a piece of their own healer within, sharing methods and tools to promote personal healing and growth. We have a table full of plenty. The more we bring to the table, the more the wealth grows, the food source multiplies, and many with a deep hunger are fed.

If You Could Choose From My Cup

"What if's" in life are things that should inspire you. They should not limit you. "What if's" should encourage and feed you! "What if's" are gifts metaphorically resembling God-candy that rains down on you, in you, through you! These two tiny words, "what if," when turned into action, fueled with intensity and desire, create a living, energetic force manifesting results. Your thoughts, desires, and dreams become your reality, tri-dimensionally, in body, mind, and soul. These two words, "what if," are a simple formula without limitations and, if chosen and acted upon, create a world of possibilities in your life. You may want to consider gifting yourself this opportunity to never limit yourself from attracting positive outcomes.

In presenting this concept to you in my opening statement, I am hoping it will it inspire you, even excite you. To further this thought-inspired action, what if I offered you a gift? What if I extended a personal invitation to choose something from my overflowing cup? The cup theory is not a new concept, and I believe that most people grasp the context of my invitation. I want you to know that I share everything I can for the good of the mankind and all living things. There is only one way to receive this gift, however: You truly need to know what to ask for. I receive these gifts from a divine source of collective energy, consciously, on every level. This energy has taught me purpose, love, and compassion. This energy goes by many names and is experienced by mankind in many modalities and methods. For me, this energy is all God, an endless source of divine workers, angels, and guides aiding our connections.

I would never, ever turn away a person who is searching for their own source of light and love. I would, with all I hold true to me and my experience, give them any gift they wished to receive from my overflowing cup! In saying this, I understand it is a tall order, but, in all truth, the God I have come to trust and with whom I have a personal relationship never, ever gives me more than I can handle. There are times, however, when the black energy of doubt seeps into my cup, lining it with black sludge that can slow down my gift-offering process. Creating a small time out, involving reflection and clearing, cleansing, and a good scrubbing of my own cup, keeps me humble and accountable.

I have come to understand that the more I give away, the more gifts appear. This is not the reason I choose to give so much away; however, it is the reason I seem to have unlimited energy and an internal tap that overflows. It is as if I have a magic store and I hold a special access key. The key unlocks the store and offers gifts to anyone asking, and the gift is then chosen out of my cup. The individual receives the exact need, craving, truth, solution, or wisdom he or she is seeking, and in this moment, we are connected. Living, loving energy channels through me, meeting the individual's needs. It is this divine-driven engine of loving power that continues to gush from my cup, providing an endless flow of loving energy, without conditions.

If I make a conscious effort to fill my cup daily, the momentum overflows with abundance and gifts to share with anyone who has a desire or wish. Whether it be words of encouragement, a message from a loved one, addressing grief, clearing old hurts, or talking about something their child did that brought them joy or pain, the more I offer my entirety, the more my cup fills. The more the cup fills, the more I need to share the flow. This momentum keeps building in perpetual motion, keeping the flow alive in each conscious, and sometimes unconscious, moment, never shutting down, filling to overflowing.

What makes me an expert, some may ask? Don't think for one moment this recording does not play through my head as my ego starts to overanalyze and tries to resume total control. This is about my soul, the healer with which I was born, and its purpose to love the world at all cost. We are all simple human beings, and we are all wonderful, spirit-filled, multi-faceted vessels of living works, living masterpieces. We all are entitled to this greatness, and we all experience fall-outs. We grow differently, and we all have gifts to offer each other. We learn this through the process of our independent living and the choices we make.

So, I ask you to ponder this: What if you decided to choose from my cup? And what if you started to fill your own cup? And what if you grew into this space of peace that consumed your day? And what if you fell in love with your cup? The "what if's" will never again limit you. Rather, they will encourage your new growth!

Share with me as I share with you! Do not be afraid to ask for something you wish, need, or desire. I realize this concept may not be for everyone; yet, I wanted you to know we can grow into anything we wish to be. Or, to further this thought, we can have all the desires of our hearts met by the simple act of self-love. Committing to self means to be open to receive the universal energy of love. We can have any desire, any experience we want. We only need to know what to wish for, and then, most importantly, "ask for it!" Give yourself permission to ask, then receive.

How Do I Fill My Own Cup?

    This chapter is about how I have come to understand how the Divine God I have come to know works in and through me. While putting thought into action in writing this book, it caught me reflecting on my first book called <u>Innerspace</u>, a very emotionally-charged experience. This book was initially directed by my spouse, acting as an agent for something bigger than he understood at the time.

    I have been given a key from my God Source that has helped me to unlock "my healer within," my soul essence, and what I have come to understand is that it is wise and patient, compassionate and flawless. This all being said, I also get to live in this flawed physical form that craves attention, food, has lust and love for living. This acceptance, in my broken state of weakness in the flesh, allows me choices that may not always be the healthiest, but are good teachers of boundaries and acceptance, structure and grace; all by accepting that my body, ego, and mind can work in conjunction with the soul existence that lives inside of me. In all honesty, my soul is much kinder, more loving, forgiving, and patient than my ego is. My ego has a job, as well, and that is to keep my common worldly sense in order. My soul is the wiser and much more experienced part of my entirety! I love that they make the best team for me and allow me to experience all the good versus the bad in my life, so that I can learn true balance. This growth serum provides knowledge for continual healing in my life lessons. You will also hear me say to many that my life this time around is teaching me new lessons to add to my already stacked portfolio; another privileged adventure of living life in a human container. My new soul brother, Keegan, tells me my name has a coded meaning. He tells me lovingly I am leaving my 'Trace' on the planet. Pretty cool perspective!

I make conscious decisions. I am committed to those decisions, working bit by bit to ensure that I am continually growing in the pain or in the joy of my decisions. In this commitment, I am accepting of my choices and the emotional realities in the experiences. In this awareness, I then get to choose how to react. My reactions are directly connected to the control valve delegating the flow of loving energy from my internal cup, which provides me with a quicker way to accept the lessons being presented, and teaching me what belongs to others with whom I am connecting. This is not the easiest thing to accomplish in the flesh, as many dynamics and emotions surface that can be of a selfish or passionate human expression. There are times when this expression can cause blocks, creating a reaction which can manifest in the exchange of negative energy between the people connecting. These interconnections are life lessons teaching us to choose how to live our lives. Claiming the truth in these moments of perfect divine timing and self-awareness encourages us to develop a healthy, wholistic, joy-filled existence.

I wish to share with you all the ways I choose to keep my cup full. I talk to God pretty much like he is attainable, always available, like a best friend, on the same level as I am on. I am made from The Divine; I am a part of divine energy; therefore, The Divine lives within me and I love that He/She surrounds me with support, providing help and hope, sending guides, angels, and teachers from the spirit side of living, as well as physical beings - dragonflies, butterflies, baby bumblebees, to mention a few. This relationship of pure, divine love flows within me.

I am in constant communication with the spirit world, as well as my human life world; they are not separated; they are combined as one existence. I can switch gears from my head to my heart or from my heart to my head without much of a thought. It just flows calmly. It is a deep understanding of the divine connection of spirit and flesh. The Divine lives in and through me, making the connection extremely personal.

Amazing things happened to me as I accepted this truth. I became a nicer, kinder person. I started to take things less personally and to claim what was mine alone. God is so wise! I guess that is why God is all divine, all knowing, all loving, all embracing, and is what we all crave deeply to return home to after our life lessons. Who loves us this much as to want to suffer with us, through us, and in us, while patiently witnessing the growth of His/Her child?

I am fully immersed in spirit connection when I focus in a quiet setting of silence, but I also hear and feel the spirit world in nature or stimulating, passionate conversation. I would say that I collectively gather moments in my life by living them in full awareness, whenever possible. This choice of living continues to fill my cup, allowing me to experience full abundance.

I am not kidding when I tell you all that I am privy to many forms of miracles. I look for them; I have come to expect them as a normal transaction in my day-to-day living. They just manifest, appear, continue to fill my cup and my heart to perpetual action and an abundance of overflow. I witness them in children, animals, the elderly, co-workers, clients, and life moments in the world around me. I sometimes take it a step farther and step out of my comfort zone, engaging with unhappy people. I have discovered in my actions that the kinder I am and the more soft-spoken allows a loving opportunity to connect in their unhappiness. This interaction between us seems to confuse them. The more confused they are, the less power they seem to hold in the negative sense. I notice that my positive state often affects their self-control. My kindness seems to stunt their negativity, defusing the energy of aggression. This is very powerful and extremely productive. However, it may be difficult to attain this kind of awareness before our human emotions ignite our ego defense mode.

I wish to share a personal healing miracle with you. It is still as clear as the moment it happened. This nugget of truth left a tiny hole in my heart resonating for a few weeks until I was able to let the lesson go, covering it with a small patch.

It so happened that I was driving to my editor's home for a visit on my way home from work, ending up at a very busy intersection of the city. On the corner, I noticed a man holding a cardboard sign that read, "I am homeless. I am hungry. Please feed me." I could feel my ego having a conversation inside of me, one of pure speculation. In that instant, I looked him over, taking in his attire and his shoes, and I judged him. I was particularly perturbed as I noticed the pair of expensive name brand of shoes he was wearing. In that moment, I made a choice that he had no need for my money. At that very same moment, I looked up and he looked into my eyes with painful wisdom beyond his circumstances. He shook his head so slightly that if I had not been so focused, I would have missed his subtle action. In this interaction between us, his heart spoke to mine and said, "Please do not worry or feel sad for me. I understand your not wanting to give to me. But I ask you, and I beg you, please do not judge me." Seriously, that was the connection and the message from his eyes, his soul, his heart. I could not shake him.

I could not take back my decision to not give him money. In that instant, I wanted more than anything to take back my choice, but the lesson for me was to let it go and let it be a lesson of the heart. Will it make me choose differently next time? Possibly not. I can only hope to be a kinder, more spontaneous, giving heart with a lot less time to judge or size up. This lesson for me was about fully accepting a person's conditions and allowing myself freedom in the choices I make, fully loving, fully embracing those lessons of treasured moments given to me. What a precious, painful gift I received that day!

Filling my cup takes dedication and loving self-care every day. I know I require a full cup, so I can be ready and willing to give anyone who shares time and space with me anything they ask for. It has been my purpose in life to continue to believe in a system that supports human beings on a level they can all attain if they reach deep within, beginning to first acknowledge, then gently shake or awaken their healer within.

Ways that I fill my cup can be little reminders of simple acts of kindness and recognition of my own self-loving worth. Another great way I fill my cup is by waking up with awareness and gratitude for the sole reason that I get to have another day of life and experience. This simple and powerful awareness of gratitude fills my cup!

There have been a few concepts this year that have changed my belief system drastically. To simplify, I have stopped expecting, with a few hiccups, and started accepting interactions that come into my daily personal life without conditions. When I am conscious of the moment, making it less about my expectation and more about the lesson of love the moments teach me, I get to choose how to address the interaction directly in that living moment. In my truth or my perception of the truth, I get to choose to react or not react. The fact remains, in my honest awareness, I get to choose if I want to invest or comment, or let it go and flow out of a place of unconditional love. This takes huge commitment, concentration, and honesty. You also get to decide to reach out and invest in a gesture of graceful kindness. This is difficult, learning how to love this deeply and not take things personally. Learning curves never cease to happen and we receive hundreds of these moments daily. It is all choice, reminding us to love ourselves and the world around us. The key ingredient is always **choice**.

I have also come to understand fully the meaning of "a safe place." For me, I realize I made a contract in spirit to partake in human form. Once born into the body, I believe I have chosen to exist in this form. The lessons I choose to experience are often hard and cause extreme moments of pain and heartache, teaching me life lessons. It is in this state of awareness I find solace in my connection with The Divine. This may seem scary to some of you, who may feel deeply you have no safe place living in this life. But please know, there is a safety net of love and your soul resonates from divine connection, calling you and comforting you. You have always been, and you will always be connected to The Divine. Your spirit never dies; it just moves on to new enlightenment through experience.

How Do I Continue to Keep My Cup Full?

How do I continue to fill my cup? I try not to look for compliments or accolades or validation from others, but I do gracefully accept them as they help to connect and validate our work and our connections to and for each other. Receiving love in all forms is like fuel for the soul, giving it an injected boost of faith. Accepting this fuel provides me courage to stay open, filling my heart with the presence of any and all connections. When working in and with spirit, time and time again, I am in an overwhelming state of awe. When we heal together in an entwined, agreed, collaborative state, we experience healing and enlightenment. Unconditional love can be addictive. Love – true, selfless love - is pure and it originates from The Divine. It has only one agenda: to love fiercely and heal greatly. Thank goodness divine energy knows we cannot survive in the whole sense without balance. Experiencing balance in our physical bodies allows us to be receptive to the teachings that ground us. Balance between body and soul calls us back home to planet earth to fully live life.

I have gratitude for the circle of healers with whom I work, who smile and send grounding to me often, as they know my balloon would take off and not return to the earth if given the chance to keep flying. They often say, "Sending grounding energy." Those in my circle know who you are. I would be in flight somewhere – in a galaxy far from the planet Earth - if it were not for your dedicated love, support, and powerful grounding gifts!

How does anyone keep their cup full? I have come to fully realize that the more I grow, the bigger my cup becomes. I collect a multitude of experiences in my day through connections, sharing, and putting my heart out there on the line. I have come to understand the fullness of my purpose. The awareness of my own needs allows me to have these the experiences and to feel the loving outcomes of giving myself permission to focus on the needs of others. I pay attention to conversations and the information that is shared with me by others. I pride myself on being 100 percent committed to hearing what people feel is important enough to share with me in their moments and to validate the person, or group of people, when they are sharing. The moment is all that matters, and it seems to make a difference.

I have come to know that the more that goes into my cup, the more gifts I receive. It seems the more I share, the more interesting new things start to gather in my cup. I have come to enjoy this process and wait with a shivering sense of anticipation as gifts start to gather and manifest in my cup. However, in saying this, there still have been serious moments in life that have caused conflicts in my human world mixing in with my spirit world. I will try to explain this further, sharing some of the human side of conflicts with you.

With every person I meet a connection is made. Some connections are instant and joy filled, while some are uncomfortable interactions filled with varying degrees of mixed emotion. We all must be honest here: good connections leave us feeling wonderful! We all crave interconnecting and wish we could have more. Bad connections leave us fearful, angry, judgmental, or even frustrated. Understanding these dynamics, an awareness starts to happen if you choose to engage in a conversation, interaction, or acknowledgement. If I can stay in a state of non-judgment, there is an opportunity to be a channel. Given permission, this allows the conduit of pure love from The Divine, connecting one soul to another.

Some people are content with just knowing what they know; they seem at peace with their lives and the purposes they have been working towards. Most children are very quick to tell you exactly what they want and what they dream about. If you listen intently and really hear the person with whom you are connecting, you soon hear with your heart and your soul source, not just your physical ears.

It usually takes a disciplined stepping out of oneself and allowing a personal connection so the person with whom you are communicating is comfortable. This state allows an experience of unconditional love, exposing desire and fullness. This experience may be foreign, leaving the person feeling an emotional response they cannot identify, possibly for the very first time. This moment of awareness can be a very powerful healing. I have witnessed this response time and time again, and this interaction confirms for me that there is something far bigger than I could understand at work. In those pure moments of connection, gifts are received. I have a full cup and I give permission for my body to be a conduit for the transfer of loving energy. This sounds like it might be painful, and at times it can be, but it is not my pain to hold. It is my purpose only to filter the pain and allow it to pass through, delivering the messages and releasing them. In those sacred moments, I get to travel home to the Light, spending some time in my own connection with The Divine who loves me.

I have come to understand healing on a whole new level. When I personally witness a healing, it is also a healing of magnificence for me. It teaches me that these gifts of wisdom are free to all who seek them. This God-love I am personally familiar with and connected to by this magical energy cord shares entirely everything loving and good in abundance, allowing me the healing that comes from sweet or bittersweet lessons.

Getting Stuck In My Cup

There have been times in my life when I have made very poor choices. Some of the choices I made changed my life in drastic ways, causing me to make even poorer choices. There have been several times when my ego has taken control and started to dominate my life. This occurs quite often when my tongue gets all caught up on words gushing from my mouth, and I wind up wishing I could take back what just came pouring out without a pause or a breath. This domino effect of pain, judgment, conflicts, and opinions are my truth in that moment. From one person to another, my passionate opinion seems to need to surface. To say I have been stuck in my cup and that it was not filling properly would be a very accurate statement. My cup does not fill when it forms cracks that start to leak.

I have come to understand the importance of getting stuck. It causes me to have no choice but to pause. Stopping in the moment forces me to find a way out of the situation. Sometimes, it is an easy solution and I just find a kinder way to address the issues, giving me the insight to turn my body on a different angle and I can slip right out of the space I was stuck in. This does take a thought process and an action. Considering less painful options may show me a different choice leading to an honest conclusion. This experience and the information attached to it allow advanced wisdom, addressing the truth, and bringing awareness. Stopping and taking the time to evaluate the place I am stuck in gives me solutions and options to make things right with my internal cup. This knowledge and wisdom within align with the love and light of the world around me. Sometimes, I hear from others, "It is not all about you." In all honestly, it truly needs to be all about you. It is a fact that to be well in a whole sense is to know how to identify and offer tools to provide a wholeness in others.

I have a history of getting stuck in several situations, and the choices I made in those situations have led me to loneliness, despair, heartache, sobbing, shaking, tears of remorse, and deep, life-changing, gut-wrenching, curl-up-in-a-ball, sheer pain. Some of the choices left me with only one thing: "my breath of life." This gift from The Divine, my prana breath connection, was the only life-sustaining thing keeping me alive in those broken moments. To this day, I welcome those *intense* lessons from the choices I made that taught me sheer determination and a whole new perspective.

It takes time to heal from being stuck in the mud, blood, dirt, sharp stones, sticks, and debris that life seems to sling at you, sometimes in a meteor shower, sometimes with snowballs, and sometimes with intense heat or cold rain. The lessons keep coming and the living keeps moving on. We sometimes are dragged along by our hair in the out-of-control mudslide we call life. It takes courage to face life full on. It takes courage to come to terms with being alone in this life and knowing that you and only you are responsible for making your life mean or count for something and choosing not to settle or get stuck. It is hard work, with as many breaks as you decide to take. If you are anything like me, you just want what you want, which sometimes causes you to get stuck in the first place. Getting unstuck is sometimes harder work than getting stuck in your cup. It takes thought, choice, action, and commitment to become unstuck.

I have learned through my reaction to pain that there are times when I choose to wallow in it. It feels good to feel sorry for my poor self, and it feels good to stroke my ego or spend time in solitude, befriending pain that my body can sometimes crave or feel justified to endure. It may all sound a bit crazy, but there are times when I admit to craving this attention, these emotions; even crazier, feeling the need to justify it as something I might deserve. I even thought that people would give me more attention if I was in a place of depression or despair; that they would feel sorry for me and want to save me from the pain or hurt by loving me; that they might carry me and my brokenness over the threshold of a safer haven, one full of love and light. I can share with you that I have waited for that white horse and white knight on more than one broken occasion. I will never say never, as life happens, and it could possibly happen to anyone, but more often than not, we need to personally take responsibility for conquering our pain and finding happiness in ourselves.

I see miracles and experience miracles every single day. As I expect they are coming, I invite them into my heart, soul, and head space. In that expectation, most often I am witness to more than one miracle; always magic, always a validation that the universe is watching and loving its beloved. My personal experience dealing with getting stuck has always ended up with me saving myself, by being open to receiving love and guidance for the sore spots in my soul from wise, healing magic from a soul sister or brother, angel, or light worker. This wiser, older part of my existence keeps me open to receiving the gifts bestowed on me by divinely connected, loving energy.

Please allow me to elaborate on the word "miracle" as I use that word often in my writing, sharing, or in reference. If you google the word, its meaning is: "An event that appears inexplicable by the laws of nature so is held to be supernatural in origin or an act of God. One that excites admiring awe; a wonderful or amazing event, act, person, or thing. An experience of awe and wonder." *(Concise Oxford English Dictionary)*

Some may ask, "Does this way of life, choosing to be a light worker, not leave you depleted?" In truth, it does, in fact, have its moments. I ask myself the same question on days when I may be physically dragging my body around like a lead hammer, or I may be in the same physical space as an energy vampire. For someone who has never heard the phrase, "spiritual vampire," I will try to elaborate for you. Psychic vampires, also known as energy vampires, are emotionally immature individuals who drain the time and energy from those around them. They are usually highly self-interested and lack empathy. The relationships they form are largely self-serving. These human beings are usually not aware on a conscious level that they are even causing harm or intending harm. I do say 'usually', but there are times when maturity and wisdom teach these beings;

yet, they then choose to continue behaving in this manner. In this case, they can become more powerful and demand more of your time and energy. It is up to us to educate ourselves and ask for protection. This can be done simply by asking God with a sincere heart to send his angels. I often call on Archangel Michael to ask to be covered in white light and love; the purest, most direct and powerful immediate answer to a request for protection.

There are times when passionate light workers are called out to work on a 24-hour clock for humanity. Often in these trying, endless hours, we can fail to deliver what we are sending. That is just called being human; however, there is bigger picture and grander force at work. It is important to note here that we are all in soul essence, yet still living in human flesh. That flesh includes a brain, and that brain houses our ego. The ego still struggles with sharing our body with our soul. Therefore, there are times when the ego says, "I need time to play and I have a need to be selfish; I want a time-out to enjoy this delicious piece of cake, or this walk on the beach in the sunset." In those times, listen and compromise. Shutting down temporarily on a regular basis is healthy.

I must admit that, in hindsight, my past few years have brought me a lot of intensity, struggling with internal growth. These challenges taught me more life-coping skills and lessons than the entire last three decades of my life. It seems that a very personal lesson two years ago started a momentum, and a downward emotional spiral had been silently escalating. It taught me that I had a deeper commitment to the word "forgiveness" and a deeper awareness of acceptance of my own personal flaws that come with being human, as well as the flaws or choices in my relationships. It taught me the true meaning of the word "sabotage" and what it means to sabotage a relationship. It taught me to try and communicate more and to let go of the expectations I was creating subconsciously about what I felt I should be receiving in return.

The experience set me free in more ways than I could ever imagine possible. When people you love hurt you more deeply than any hurt you could ever imagine possible and you survive that hurt, you grow differently. The secret for me was to take control of the emotions immediately and take care and nurture my hurt. I learned through this process that the quicker I dealt with the hurt, the easier it was to release the heartache. It was really a simple deduction of action and a plan to move forward. Truly, if you want the secret of happiness, I totally believe that the act of forgiving completely sets you free. This action of complete and total forgiveness allows you to keep the memory as a reference, tucked away to teach you that true forgiveness is unconditional.

This is the best part: You forgive the ignorance of the infliction and you still get to hold on to the lesson. Whatever its context, this life lesson taught you awareness, inspired self-love, and new internal growth. Does this mean you will not suffer the aftershocks of heartache? No, it truly does not. It does mean, however, that you are quicker to heal, identify your part in the action, and move on and up. You will still feel heart-bruising and insecurity until the wound heals. The scar tissue is just there to remind you that you have grown past this, and it also reminds you to sidestep that sensitive area of your heart and move forward. Your soul heart space has many chambers, rooms, and colour-coded file folders. Forgiving the hurt and filing it away in the folder for Experience or Forgiveness allows you to identify, claim, and acknowledge your actions, giving you room in your heart to make new life and love experiences for you. It does take time to recover from devastation of any kind. Give yourself the time you need, but do not linger too long. The sooner you forgive, the quicker you will heal. Forgiveness is the answer to every single problem. This starts with forgiving yourself, then finding the strength to forgive others.

Virtues In My Cup

Virtues, for me when applied to practice, give me clarity. In my research, I have come to honour and respect each and every one of the virtues below. I hope you feel the same way when you allow yourself a deeper understanding of the real meaning and the intent of the virtue when applied to your everyday life.

The following description of virtues briefly explains both the positive and the mirrored side of the virtue. Keep in mind, everything in life pertaining to being human in the full sense gives you an opportunity to choose either experience. How else would we know the difference between positive, negative, black, or white, if not for the grand lesson of experience?

Virtues in my cup include:

- CHASTITY
- MODERATION
- CHARITY
- DILIGENCE
- PATIENCE
- KINDNESS
- HUMILITY

CHASTITY

Chastity is one of the seven virtues that apply to a person and his or her sexuality. Chastity means you take your sexual desires and apply them to fit the definition of love. Contrary to popular belief, the word "chastity" does not mean "no sex." Chastity means that a relationship is free from using each other as objects or for pure pleasure. Chastity applies to the rules and the guidelines that you and your partner mutually set forth within your relationship. It means approaching each other with love and desire, not with an unhealthy obsession for the dark, perverse sexual desire, which would be the mirror of chastity, or lust.

MODERATION

Moderation is one of the seven virtues that can be the most difficult to live out. Moderation means striking a balance between the things we enjoy and the things we need to do. It means we balance play, work, and family. Moderation means we focus on every relationship in our lives and try to bring each of them to a balance. It means we do not forsake work for play or play for work. The dark mirror to moderation is gluttony or the overindulgence in all things.

CHARITY

Charity is opening your heart to the world and the universe. It means giving of yourself to someone or something in need. Charity does not mean financial giving or material giving. It can mean giving of your time, yourself, and your love. Charity that comes from your heart shows the true picture of the light of the universe. It shows that you have compassion and love for all those around you. Having the spirit and the light to give of yourself without expecting anything in return is the true meaning of charity. While charity is unselfish and giving, the dark mirror of charity is greed and the obsessive desire to have and to be more than anyone else. One who is greedy cannot also love.

DILIGENCE

To be diligent is to be wise and alert in all your actions. It means to work hard, with both enthusiasm and attention to detail. It means to approach a task with persistence and decisiveness. Diligence means you have the capability to harness the powerful light of the universe and to realize your full potential, as you budget your energy in the tasks set before you. Diligence is a necessary quality in this life as you face hurdles or trials set before you. Diligent people do not give up. The dark side of the mirror of diligence is sloth, or uncaring and laziness. Slothful people expect others to do everything for them.

PATIENCE

You cannot experience love without patience. If you are consistently impatient with another person, you feel little love towards that person. To be patient is to be enlightened by the universe and to be able to persevere under trying circumstances. Patience is to act towards others in all situations without resorting to anger, frustration, or annoyance. Your level of patience is the level of trial your character can take before you begin to act in a negative manner. The dark mirror for patience is anger. Anger can be quick and harsh, and learning to curb your anger can be a difficult task. Unresolved, deep-seated anger prevents a person from experiencing or living a full life based on the other virtues of love, charity, kindness, and humility.

KINDNESS

Those who exhibit kindness have a sincere appreciation and joy for what they already have. This virtue of kindness allows you to rejoice for and with others. Kindness teaches sharing with others instead of wanting another's life, relationship, or possessions for their own. Kind people are considerate of others and realize that kindness not only reflects the light of the universe; it also reflects the light of love within you. It is another example of love and harmony within yourself and your universe. The dark mirror of kindness is envy. Envy creeps up and wraps around you, whispering the desire it believes you should have for the possessions of others.

HUMILITY

When asked, "What are the seven virtues," humility is often the hardest to remember because it can be the hardest to live out. "Humility," is the "antithesis," or direct opposite, of arrogance and pride. Those who live their lives in humility are never boastful or proud. Humility is being respectful of others. Being humble allows us to place others before ourselves in all ways. Humility allows us to meet the needs of others. The dark side of humility is pride, vanity, and ego, all characteristics which caused the downfall of both Lucifer and man in the eyes of God.

This chapter has been a very challenging chapter for me to write, as I kept coming back to the word "Karma." I, myself, have misused the intentions of this word and the meaning in and throughout my lifetime. You have often heard statements like "Karma is a bad thing," or "What goes around comes around," basically meaning that Karma will get you in the end, giving you what you deserve, retribution for some perceived wrong. Or, you personally may even be holding out to bear witness to a wrongful intention made right, enjoying fully the painful lesson being taught and received through so-called Karma. I, myself, have been guilty of this kind of mentality.

This mythical concept that there is something called Karma lurking in the dark, ready to strike at you because you choose to be mean-spirited or intentionally inflict harm and pain on another, is, in my experience, simply not true. It would be entirely more accurate for me to say something that has come to be my truth. I live through the experience of my own intentions, receive the actions of my intentions, until my lessons are learned. If it is my intention to inflict pain or suffering, I am usually the receiver of pain and suffering. Karma teaches me valuable lessons of learning actions from family or lineage connected sometimes for many generations, even past lifetimes. Repeating the lesson causes a loop of repetitive patterns until we are strong enough to break the cycle. Awareness replaces the lesson; growth happens; forgiveness is achieved, and we now have room, internal space, to move forward.

Let me try to clarify what I mean when I say "inflict pain or wish revenge." The intention itself is something you may passionately wish justice for. It is something people, myself included, tend to dwell on that makes us feel someone is going to get what is coming to them. This kind of intention steals our power. We hand it over and give it freely away to intend or inflict pain or harm or justification on someone for something we were personally affected by: actions or a word of gossip that felt like a personal attack leaving one hurt and vulnerable, raw and angry, causing the emotion of embarrassment and inflicting pain. It is my strong belief that when we hold on to this version of "Karma," we are not modelling the virtues described above and living our lives as the best version of ourselves.

For me, virtues are impactful words of wisdom, beacons of hope, guiding me to the source and true meaning of unconditional love. They encourage me and remind me that I am human and need to be diligent and truthful, kind and honest. If I can maintain my own integrity, I have a clearer perspective to be honest externally to the people who are drawn to connect with me. This intention and commitment stabilize my internal cup, allowing an abundance of connected universal love and wisdom.

Seasons Of My Cup

If I could paint you a picture of my internal cup, I would start at the top, painting all four seasons. In this chapter I will attempt to paint a picture of how I feel and what the seasons mean to me. I will share with you my own gratitude life lessons and how I have come not only to understand the cycle of the seasons, but also how to get the very most value out of them. Over the years, this has become my perception and my understanding of the cycle of life, beautiful Mother Earth, memories, and lessons our beloved planet has taught me; mixing my favorite traditions that attach to the seasons in description of colours, examples, and a few of my favorite things.

I will start by sharing with you my favorite season: fall. Landscape, foliage, a collage of leaves, the sweet taste of hot apple cider, the texture of baked, buttery pepper squash, the aroma of fresh-out-of-the-oven pumpkin pies, turkey and savory dressing – just think about it! I love Thanksgiving, mostly for the simplicity and deep reverence of gratitude deeply seated in the core of my heart space. It is a holiday designated to give thanks: no gifts exchanged; time spent with family in an intimate gathering. These were my childhood memories of Thanksgiving. There is no added stress for me on this weekend, and it falls in my favorite season. It feels good to be thankful and to share that time and connection. For me in my adult life, it has not always been celebrated with my immediate family; in fact, that is rarely the case. I have come to know that just because you are not related by flesh and blood does not mean you cannot have people in your life whom you call your family. Who is to say you cannot share this same rich experience of giving and being kind and thankful in other choices and non-traditional ways? I choose to be happy on this weekend and thankful, no matter who sits at my table.

If you want to enrich your own cup in this season and embrace the spirit of Thanksgiving, you might try doing something kind for a stranger or a neighbour. Consider serving dinner at a homeless shelter and enjoy the rewards of this action. Enjoy the surprise and feelings of sheer, uninhibited ecstasy when sharing your true core self with others. We are all indirectly connected to each other in spirit, coming from the same energy of life. Consider opening your heart to a stranger who may really need an act of random kindness. Commit to visiting a lonely person in an assisted living seniors' facility or a hospital or hospice, reading them a story or just holding their hand. Spending time with the elderly can be extremely rewarding and surprisingly interesting!

Literally, in a nutshell, fall is the season to gather. We could take a cue from the wisdom of animals who instinctively gather and start planning for the impending winter. This is a collective time to celebrate the harvest of your year, giving some thought to what you gained through the spring and summer. It is a time to be good to all mankind, a gesture of true gratitude. Your internal gratitude will gain momentum in your cup as you continue to pay attention and you witness the squirrels working away as a team, gathering and sharing, dividing the fruits of the land. They are on a mission, instinctively driven, working together for survival. We all can learn much from nature.

Collectively, we also gather, bundle, and store in many different forms. As human beings, we are aware of the need to prepare for the changing of the seasons. Fall represents the season of beauty found in dying for me. It is a time of reflection and a time of wholeness and continuous awareness of change and gratitude.

The second season I would paint on my cup would be spring. I love the anticipation of what is coming into new growth. It seems to me that this season is the most intense and the shortest. It is usually not the most pleasant season to experience physically, for me. Spring can be mostly damp, cold rain; life waking up and thawing out. This season brings new birth, nudging nature's sleeping babies. New buds start their formation, slowly and steadily, growing into the fingers, extending arms, joining roots. Take a few moments to sit silently. Allow yourself to close your eyes. Listen! You can hear growth all around you! Vibrant spring flowers have very short lives. These chosen flowers, however, make splashes of deep richness combined with intense aroma. These flowers remind me of nova stars, their brilliance leaving a longing for their essence, lingering in memories long after they are gone.

Everything is more intense in the spring season: rich smells of raw earth, and the knowledge that all life is returning from the state of hibernation. This season defines new growth and depth for my body, filling my cup with joyful anticipation of all the wonders of summer. When I think about what colours I would paint this section of my cup, I would choose pale yellow, soft pinks, shades of green, and violet. The gifts I would add would be Easter eggs and straw baskets, fresh mint, sage, and frankincense oil. The beauty of your cup comes from whatever you decide to include. The secret is simply creating it and filling it with whatever makes you appreciate this short, vibrant season. This may teach you to fully embrace the essence of spring, awakening new birth in your full-on, conscious life.

The season of summer brings the taste of salt from the ocean on my lips and the feel of sand between my toes on the shore; the brisk, cold, crisp bite of welcome and reality from our many Great Lakes; feeling your whole being enveloped by the wind and the sun as they join together, creating colour and warmth on your skin; summer fun; peace on the beach near the water's edge. I find my inner peace in the middle of summer. It is warm and puts me in a total state of contentment as the sun kisses my head, warming my entire body. We have had many incredible experiences in this season over the past several years. Together, we have lived by the water and on the water. We have ridden into sunsets and sunrises on a motorcycle. If I were to paint this section of my cup, it would be varied shades of blues and sand; it would be dark orange sunsets and tiny white, puffy clouds; wavy, blue water and hues of gold with slivers of silver.

I might suggest at this point to go within and meditate on the elements that constructively bring life to our seasons. On many levels they provide natural, home-grown nutrients; living tools to promote internal and external healing. Respecting our Mother

Earth through conscious awareness of the world's awakening may help to keep your mind acute and responsive.

Sleeping on the water is like being rocked to sleep in the arms of The Divine in its purest form, love in action. Peace happens. There are times when we just sit in solitude and let the universe embrace us, with water underneath us and stars above us, suspended in time. In these precious moments, I feel an overwhelming presence of the universe joining us as one vast connection. This kind of experience always leaves me with deep emotions. I never want it to end! I experience a knowing and gratitude, a true sense of awe! My emotions are heightened and I am on the verge of tears, trying to grasp how big the universe is and placing my existence in it. Then, a calm voice stills my heart and simply says, "Because you are mine and I created all this for you to enjoy."

Summer is my time-out season. I love harder, play harder, and spend more time outside than inside. I enjoy the earth, the heat, the wind, the water, in as much abundance as I can receive every day. It is a wonderful season, bringing sunshine, vacations, connections. This season subliminally allows us to take time out. It is a season that leaves us aching on so many levels for down time and a chance to play, to be young, and to explore possibilities. Many people do not want summer to end – ever! They are not aware on a deeper level why they feel this way. That takes work, focus, gratitude, and awareness, as well as time and courage to understand and accept the learning, gracefully and happily accepting that all the best things, like the best part of summer, come and go. It is only going without it that allows us to understand and accept beauty of this season!

My least favorite season is winter – for several reasons. For many, winter represents a season of dormant state and suspended time, but for me, winter is my personal season of learning and hard work. In all honesty, it is my most productive growing season. I have had more brokenness and healing in winter than in any other season of the year. In past years, I would shut down and close myself off from the world, taking a break from everyone and everything. I thought I could not grow if I did not shut down. I believed, if I sat remaining open, that another gift from the Spirit would be added to the gifts previously provided to me. This was a huge misconception. I would tell my clients that I was not seeing anyone from November to April, which did not serve the purpose of my light work. However, what it did teach me was that by choosing to shut myself down, I was setting conditions on myself and on my clients. This was a huge moment of hurtful truth. This taught me that you are either all in or all out. It also taught me that neither choice was wrong or right, it was just a choice: to grow with divine love without conditions or to remain in the space I was in.

In hindsight, I did receive gifts in this time of shutting down. I did also set conditions. Those conditions sent a message to the clients with whom I work that I was not available, physically or emotionally, for them or myself. How does one truly learn unconditional love when one sets conditions for all? One day last winter, I heard a voice say, "Tracey, stop trying to save the world. You no longer need to search out and reach out to brokenness. Brokenness will reach out and find you, and you will be available anywhere and everywhere when this happens. You no longer need a scheduled time-out. You can always take a time out when you need it."

True to this statement, that is what happens to me now. I do not reach out, offering to assist. I wait and they come, in all shapes, sizes, forms, and needs. There are times in this open way of living, after being witness to the miracle of healing in a session, that I do reach out if I feel someone is in need and I do touch base, offering love and assistance. Even in the knowing, growth and gifts are granted to me while waiting with an open, honest heart and a cup full of love. I have come to trust the universe and The Divine completely. I do not hold on to my lessons. I have no valid need for them to take up room, crowding my internal flow. I find it is easier to just accept them and embrace them. This does not mean that they are not very painful lessons. These lessons teach me value, allowing my dharma (the principal of cosmic order) to coincide with my personal life choices, creating healthy boundaries and, without a doubt, clarity.

It is in this winter season that all this truth resonates within me. I sleep on a deeper level in this season than any other. This season gives us reason to be snug and warm and enjoy mugs of hot chocolate, thick blankets, and cozy fires. I have come to embrace the beauty and the boldness of this season.

Painting my winter cup would look like a window that had been visited by Jack Frost. It would be a beautiful icicle masterpiece, one of a kind, a hint of winter's cold breath, a tiny spot of sun peeking through the top pane. This season gives me many reasons to feel the true, hard-earned ache of growth spreading through my being on every level, persistently nagging me to keep growing towards true awareness, true gratitude, in our moments of frozen solitude.

If you chose to paint your own Cup Full of Seasons, what would you paint? Explore your heart and your soul; paint your internal, overflowing cup; bring it to life; take all the time in the world to paint your personal experience.

Drops In My Cup

    I want to talk about how one might define a drop in your cup. I thought I would start by sharing with you some of the moments that define how I have come to collect drops to keep my cup full. They can be big, life-changing moments of freedom or the discovery of tiny moments that matter to you. These fragments of full acceptance, no matter how large or how small, are the drops in our cups. I will pull out a few precious drops to share with you. These drops taught me service, purpose for my life, and the lessons of love.

    Joe and I had the great fortune of being invited by dear friends to take a spur-of-the-moment, whirlwind trip to Paris. It was a Tuesday at the end of August 2016. We landed in Paris and met up after a three-hour power nap. The first thing we did was head out onto the street to find a café. We enjoyed a delicious snack of stacked tomato slices with thick slices of fresh mozzarella cheese, sundried tomato, olive oil, and balsamic vinegar. The café was located on a busy street, full of Paris life and all the latest fashion. I was trying to take it all in at once: the place, the city, the reality of what had happened in less than a day. Sensory overload! Right beside the café was a quaint, homemade chocolate shop. The shopkeeper was kind, spoke English very well, and even made some funny comments. He asked what had brought us to Paris. We both smiled and said, "We came for dinner."

    We left the café and carried on to the Arc de Triomphe, and then the Eiffel Tower. Even from a distance it is beautiful. It is almost like you can reach out and break a piece off the leg and eat it. It is like steel lace. As we were leaving the Eiffel Tower, we saw a group of monks from Cambodia. I ran straight over and asked permission to have my photo taken with the monks. I was beyond excited, and as I reached out to touch a young monk to get closer for the photo, I instantly felt that I had disturbed sacred God-space. An elderly monk came over directly and spoke to me, asking me to please not touch. I immediately dropped my hand, thanking him for reminding me and asking for forgiveness. It was granted in a smile and gesture; the photo was taken and bows were exchanged. "Namaste." That experience stood out for me, teaching me about their choice to be dedicated to the chastity of their communion with The Divine.

The Louvre's rich history was the entrance to another world, through a gateway into another space, place in time. Every piece of history held a secret and a story. Every room, every marble step, every piece of art represented a learning opportunity. The experience alone of "just being present" felt like I might combust from the inside out! All the history, lineage, and stories still live in this building. I walked over to the Mona Lisa and just stood in her presence. It felt like I was home in a sense; a feeling of familiarity and unity. I rested on her face and smiled a full breath of satisfaction. There are so many stories that have circulated over the years, setting out timeframes and facts on how Leonardo DaVinci came to paint our beloved Mona Lisa, but for me it would make little or no difference. I have just come to recognize women in all our beauty in her face and her demeanor. When I saw her for the first time, my immediate thought was: There you are! You have been inside me my entire life! To truly appreciate an emotion, it must be felt, accepted, cherished, recognized, raw, real, beautiful. Mona Lisa's smile is a smile of earned knowledge, wisdom, heartache, and mystery, which drew me in and held me close.

While this 'quick trip' was a most unusual experience, it has something to say about just being spontaneous and jumping in with both feet, even if you do not have all the details. Having faith is imperative in this kind of scenario. It simply means you choose to trust the unknown and know that there will be a positive experience.

Keeping drops in your cup takes commitment to being consciously aware that there are drops to gather. Drops come in all shapes, forms, sizes, experiences, interactions, and, of course, actions. We can choose to fill our cup daily with all kinds of moments we experience. We also get to choose which drops remain contained, which drops we choose to share, or which drops we will offer to others.

Drops in your cup are not just the moments that bring you the deepest joys, like finding true love, travelling, getting married, having children and grandchildren, all of which are joy-filled moments creating purpose. There are also huge drops of heartache, personal devastation, and pain that you choose to experience, as well, that create important learning opportunities and assist in the development of who you ultimately choose to become and what drops you choose to keep. Being balanced and grounded are part of the lessons represented by these drops in your cup. Like most treasures, the experience, the story, and the memory are drops in our cup that teach us what to keep or repeat, or which drops to use as tools and guides to live a balanced life.

I know this whole concept takes time to develop, cultivate, and build your reservoir. I also know for a fact that The Divine to whom we are connected doubles your pleasure, meeting you every step of the way. Soon, you start living a life receiving nourishment from both this human world and the energy world of the soul. Your wealth in both worlds increases. You have more to keep. You take on more knowledge. You grow beyond your expectations.

I believe every new day brings magic. I practice first by acknowledging this to be true in the tiniest thing. I was sitting outside shortly after my mother-in-law transitioned this year. I had my eyes shut and I was sitting in the hot sun, warming my face, thawing my heart. I missed her. I felt warm tears running out of the corner of my eye and, suddenly, I felt a small flutter of a movement on my pointer finger. I slowly opened my eyes to discover a small baby bumblebee, sitting, waiting, and resting. It stayed in that exact spot for well over a full minute, maybe even two. Time stood still, both of us adjusting to this foreign intimacy. Then, I heard her on my heart, "Honey, baby steps. This is new space for me; this is new space for us; baby steps." The baby bee, as if on cue, flew away.

Sometimes, we recognize drops in a one-on-one conversation; sometimes, in listening to the burden on someone's heart. Sometimes, it is in nature. Drops can fall from many places, filling us, always teaching, always guiding us home to divine love. Being aware is crucial.

Drops in your cup are something I encourage you to accumulate, store up, fill up, rejoice with, rejoice in. Think big, plan, set goals, keep secrets; allow those secrets to grow inside you; pull those secrets out and reflect on them; rejoice in your journey of discovering you, allowing your secrets to assist you in developing your own self-loving contract. Be spontaneous! It is an incredible rush of satisfaction that will break routine, bring joy to your life, and fill your cup with new drops. Dream everyday about things you want to do, places you want to visit, mountains you want to climb. Break routine; go for a long walk in nature; book a trip to see a place you have wanted to see. Visit a sick relative; do something for another person in need and never let them know it was you. This is truly about keeping your cup full drop by drop.

Keeping love drops in my cup flowing freely has been a very conscious decision for me. How can I offer solutions and healing if I do not buy into this way of self-love, which supports me in both my healing room and outside of it? I work hard every day on being aware of the drops that continue to fill my cup, welcoming all lessons needed to keep my cup consistently balanced. Gratitude is key to this, and gratitude is something I am highly conscious of. It is a mindful, daily practice. It is a daily ritual that can take only a few weeks of consistent practice to incorporate into your life.

Did I mention how hard this way of living life can be? Well, this brings me back to reminding you to keep those drops in your cup as full as possible; reminding you of your possibilities; you have a lifetime of references. I am grateful for all that happens in my day. So many things happen that I would be writing forever, so instead, I will just sit and digest how awesome my life is and how grateful I truly am. It is interesting that I have become far more aware of my purpose in this life; more than ever I dreamed. One Sunday, it so happened I had six free hours. I walked around my house at a loss of what to do with myself. For the first time in many months, I had some free time and decided to go for a walk. As it happened, God spoke to my heart and I listened as he directed me to a person who needed to feel loved. I was rewarded for my obedience three blocks later. And so it goes, on and on in my days as I struggle with being human, learning personal pain and sacrifices, guilt and selfish acts of self-preservation, finding joy in all my moments, good and bad. And then I know I would never have it any other way!

I have this internal fountain of radiant energy that never quits. This fountain reminds me of the one we stood beside in Paris. It is the elaborate center of a twisted story. I am standing underneath the fountain, holding on to a cherub suspended by its wings but attached by its heart and chest. The water from the fountain gains its power at my feet, and I feel the pressure building from the base, pushing all the water from the bottom, gushing its way up the center column. I wait for the water pressure to accumulate as the water explodes and starts to pour over the rim, drop by endless drop. This waterfall saturates me from head to toe, filling me, cleansing me, refreshing me, bringing new life. I am accumulating drops in my cup, ready and willing to share the wealth with those brave enough to stand in the fountain of life beside me.

Ego-Friendly Drops In Your Cup

It is interesting, what we decide to give power to and voice out loud. Hearing the truth in that voice encourages us to speak outside our comfort zone. In those vulnerable moments of expressing your thoughts and passion, your guard is down, gloves are off, fully exposing the veneer we all mask so perfectly. This façade of truth on our exterior can also support the wall of self-protection we all build around our internal heart.

An example comes to mind. Not so long ago, I had an opportunity to connect over coffee and a deep discussion with two different kinds of people; one from a soul (spiritual) perspective and one from the world's (Ego) perspective, both bringing valid points of view to the stimulating conversation. The depth of this combined information stayed undigested in my heart chakra. Our discussion not only consisted of ingesting coffee and food for the body, but also food for the soul. I am still digesting slowly. Some of the truth in our deep discussion left my ego with a bit of a bruise. Sharing different, passionate experience when not of the same mindset can stop you in your tracks for a spell, giving you time to reflect on information you may never have considered. This was the case for me on this occasion.

During our visit, we started to talk about the benefits of the different educational systems we are privy to if we choose to learn, accept, and grow. My friend was talking about a book called <u>The Power of Now,</u> and he told us he had taken some time out to explore the concept of being focused on presence, so he can be more mindfully present. As he was speaking from his heart, I experienced clarity. My other lovely friend was also able to express her truth and hear differently with her heart. She received the information on a less personal level. Truly hearing these points of view adjusted my concepts and thoughts involving my ego and soul. It taught me that we are all, every one of us, on a different stage in this journey, and that contracts are personal, exciting, and should be respected, even if not understood.

I suddenly had this moment of being able to express in words and with complete clarity the healing and growing in the conversation. I had believed that I had to suppress my ego to hear my soul, but that is simply not my reality any longer. As I witnessed and we conversed from the true depths of our hearts, it all came together for me, revealing a personal growth. We can accept each other without any expectation for the sheer fact of the differences that separate us.

I believed for many years that I was supposed to suppress my ego; however, I was forgetting how much my ego helps sustain my life, i.e. by sending messages to keep my body safe. I was mindfully aware that without my ego reminding me when to eat, drink, sleep, or shut down, my soul would simply not be able to experience the life that it was meant to experience in a human, living being. In this awareness, my ego reminded me that it is not the enemy; in fact, it is a partner my soul needs to count on day in and day out, moment by glorious moment. How much easier is it to just accept this equal partnership, this union of ego and soul. This reality, for me, creates more happy pockets to gather healing drops, accepting and sustaining life as one united force of healing love.

In this agreed partnership of ego and soul, we consider the marriage of these two separate life forces residing in this one body. If we join forces, with the two creating a dedicated and respected team, we can then nurture our divine essences with richly anointed, ego-friendly drops. This saturation of combined ego and spirit can live in wholeness with the combination of compassion and logic.

In reflection, it seems to me that without equal respect, consideration, acknowledgment, love and awareness for both, ego and soul, it would be impossible to attain a higher frequency of love and light. What does manifest in the two uniting forces? A complete, whole understanding of unconditional acceptance for each other. This acceptance, then, creates an acute awareness in conjunction with divine love, as one unified force of living, loving, physical, spiritual energy. If we become one, we will understand the transformation of becoming connected to The Divine. We all get to be ourselves in this connection of oneness, and we all get to keep our own thumbprint that is unique to each of us. We never lose a thing in this connection. We all gain, collectively, committed to a loving purpose of unity.

Fractures In Your Cup

You may have an interest in what this title might be suggesting. Well, by now I am pretty sure you all know I am referring to your physical body, your soul, your spiritual body, as your cup. When you use the word "cup" you get a picture of what a cup looks like, feels like, and the purpose for most cups - to fill them with something we can all use. A cup can be container to store items; it can be used to fill us with sustenance; or it can be a work of art, displayed as an object of crafted beauty.

I suggest that you to take a moment and close your eyes and choose your cup. Look at it; see how it feels in your hands; experience the way you mold around it. Does it fit? Is it too big? Too small? Does it feel foreign or detached? Feel it! Feel the emotions stirred internally when you are visualizing your cup. Do you feel happy? Is it warm and inviting, or cold and hard? Does it have age marks or stains? Is it white and clean? Is the cup made of clay? Porcelain? Ceramic? Is it pretty? Is it delicate? Really take a moment and create the cup your body represents as your vehicle, your vessel, sustaining your life.

My hand-painted teacup has intricately placed red roses adorning its full body and matching saucer. My cup is aged and has gold filigree along the rim and saucer's edge. The shape is not round, but rather square with rounded corners, and the saucer's edge is scalloped. My cup and saucer are a delicate set of fine porcelain, thin and strong. My cup is everything I am not from an external perspective, but this cup is everything I believe to be my internal truth. This is how I see and feel myself on the inside. In fact, although my internal cup is the exact opposite of my external personality, my often bull-in-a-china-shop, boisterous splash of "here I am" colour is annoying even to myself! In saying this, there are times I swear I have a split personality. Honestly, there are times when I feel like I am living fully in two completely separate worlds simultaneously. It is surprising what we try to cover up or hide because we don't want people to know our true selves. We avoid this vulnerability by strengthening our defenses and becoming exceptional deflectors. It is even more painful to admit we sometimes overextend our giving nature, so the receivers feel more beholden to the connections, bonds, or relationships we have built together.

Exposing myself makes me feel vulnerable, but if I do not expose myself, how I can expect anyone else to do so? Exposing oneself is the first step to real wholeness, which brings me to the title of this chapter. How does one put a value on their internal cup? How much is your cup worth to you? Do the cracks represent wisdom? The chips missing - are they lessons learned and shared like fine pieces glued back together, reinforced with attached value? In all fairness, the world would devalue a cup and saucer in this kind of shape. I, however, look for these signs and symbols, as I see them as treasures. Time and time again, I recognize and find value, beauty, and wisdom in the stress fractures in people's cups. God has granted me the wisdom to help people glue and mend their own stress cracks. I guide and facilitate these personal healings, lessons of growth, from bits of unproductive past lessons. I believe with everything I am that the wisdom we attain in this life is a process, and that process is, indeed, of value.

These stress fractures all represent a victory in the specific experiences or choices made. This has taught defined placement and self-respect in my growth, aiding me to recognize my chosen path. Metaphorically, the more cracks, the more experience; the more experience, the more growth; the more growth, the more completion of the lesson chosen. The cracks are like badges of honour.

The stress fractures in my cup have come to serve me well. They have held up through the test of time. The fractures still expose the beauty of the design, adding worth and leaving a rich patina to the aged wisdom. The porcelain never loses its vibrant colour in the rose pattern, nor does the cup change its shape. Surprisingly, the lines of stress just add to the design of the cup, and no matter how many cracks are on the surface, the insides stay functional and intact, still serving the purpose of holding sustenance to sustain my life. This purpose keeps filling my cup with love, quenching all my thirst!

Layers In My Cup

As I continue to grow in this life and look back fondly - or not so fondly - over the last six decades of living, I tend to see some patterns that repeated until I got the lessons or the messages. Sometimes, it strikes me in my funny bone that it seems to take so long to get some things that are just, in hindsight, so simple.

When I was a wee little girl, I use to get so frustrated that no one seemed to hear my voice. I quickly learned how to get what I needed by action or distraction, thus forming the first layer of my cup. For the first few years of my life I think I was depressed, and I think it was because I felt suppressed. Of course, my parents had no idea. They were so young and overwhelmed, with a large family to care for and so many mouths to feed, that they must have just been on auto pilot.

To describe the first layer of my life, in retrospect, it was like a thick, pea soup fog that settled in and formed my existence. Surviving in this phase of my life would be the most descriptive word. It was beyond frustrating for me that my hands and my tongue were tied so often. I always felt I knew more of why I was supposed to be here on this planet; however, it was hard to find anyone who understood my calling. I felt lonely, but not alone. I developed a simple understanding or a craving for education and learning, but was far more receptive to another educational system not from this world. I never really took an interest in world events, history, mathematics, or any school subject that was not of a creative nature.

I can only assume during all these primary years that some of my teachers wanted to ship me away to a school that taught a different kind of curriculum; however, that was not my lesson. My poor parents probably had a few heated conversations behind closed doors about my well-being, just trying to understand their foreign child's way of reasoning. My dad was just so dang happy that I even graduated grade eight. I remember some white-knuckled nights with my dad losing his patience, trying to teach me something that to him seemed so easy and simple, but baffled me beyond words. It just did not compute. I probably should have been educated in the Creative Arts school system that, in my time, was nonexistent, and certainly not one our family could finance. The curriculum of child creativity being the premise, the root, of Montessori schools for instance, probably would have sky-rocketed my whole being.

This difficult way of living, for me, caused a lot of conflict internally, as well as externally. I lashed out and, at times, caused tension and fights with my siblings. I must admit, even to myself, just talking about these memories can still make me feel sad and confused. Lingering too long on these difficult memories can still cause deep pain. The effects have left scars that still surface if triggered from time to time. I am aware of these triggers and continue to work on healing them.

The second layer of my cup is made up of soft pinks; pale, faded, patched blue jeans; and creamy yellow. It was a time in my life when I was somewhat empowered and somewhat secretive. It was the early 1970s, I think. The first five years of the '70s for me were all about being a free spirit and not being responsible. However, I was raised to be a good girl, and thank goodness some of that surfaced, stopping or stalling my disappointing or disrespecting my parents. Like myself, I would suspect many teenagers lost that fear as they moved into those powerful, sexually-charged, peak years of senior high school. Those years gave me a first glimpse of the power I had in controlling my own destiny, as well as the power sexuality had in my personal experience with the male species - boyfriends in particular; all friends in general.

To say this was a time in my life that brought me personal pleasure and satisfaction would be correct. It also taught me varying degrees of heartache that set the course for the next three decades of my life. I did not really pay attention to the curriculum that could have, or maybe should have, given me tools to build a better future for myself and stabilize my security in life. I was too interested in the other parts of life I thought I had missed out on. I certainly had more freedom in high school than ever before and a wider variety of friends. It is probably a good thing my parents were so strict and demanded such respect from me or I might have fallen harder and not worked so hard trying to find my way back home.

I did suffer emotionally in my eleventh grade and that set me back, taking several years to bring it all home for me. Timing is always important on any journey, and I guess it is well-put to say, "The moment you stop trying is the moment you start dying." I also think it is fair to say it is okay to have a spiritual death or two, or more, while still living. I call these soul deaths - a heartache you can only describe as death and deep loss, followed by a knowing or lesson, and then redemption through a great, peaceful understanding. It is possibly better described as a growth inside your soul rather than your body. It is like your soul speaks and understands through your body's heartaches, an all-encompassing, universal language.

The next layer of my cup would be somewhat interesting. It is layered with baby powder, baby formula, cabbage rolls, Kraft Dinner, vacuum cleaners, and black shadows of exhaustion under my eyes due to a zombie state of nonexistence! Just perpetual motion, without sleep or thinking; no awareness or considering that there is anyone else in the universe. It was a time in my life when I felt fear more than at any other time, despair more than any other emotion. Survival was the only thing I focused on.

I am sure I did it all wrong back then. I know I was a failure not only to myself, but also to the people for whom I was supposed to be responsible. It was awful. For them, for me, it was a place in time I would not ever want to repeat, but if I could go back and change it, knowing the devastating outcomes, I most definitely would. Being honest with yourself in this moment of complete truth, would you not, if given the opportunity, consider one or two things you might change? If you were granted a day, a step back in time, knowing what you know now, would most people not choose differently? I don't think there is a person alive who, if given that opportunity, would not go back and try to do something different. We all have made choices over which we have guilt or crushed hearts. Do we eventually come to terms with those outcomes and learn, grow, and heal from these choices? One would hope so, but keep in mind, all choices have accountability, and all choices, in the end, teach us the lessons we set out to learn. Consequences are essential in the life lesson of choice. What remains is the learning, the insight that comes with your lesson.

This lesson has every single bit to do with me and the way I take things personally. Even more interesting to me is that if I take something personally, then clearly, I have not learned the lesson. Believe me, it is not very pretty and disappoints me greatly that I am still so judgmental and selfish. I guess the acceptance of this truth makes it easier to just let the lesson unfold, as it is in my space and face for a reason. Human beings are often very hard on themselves, especially when they start to not only see the light, but also come to whole and full understanding of the light's origin. This allows one, with whole self, to walk towards the light, encompassing, embracing where we are all from: living, collective consciousness!

A thin layer of salt and pepper line my cup in this layer. It is strange that I feel younger stepping slightly over the threshold of my sixth decade than the past two decades combined. I suppose this growth is earned and healthy. I take so many things far less personally, unless of course I know they belong to me. I choose quicker response times to address issues, claim what is mine, and find closure. I move on in my days with a certain earned peace in my heart and joy in my step, with pure, honest acceptance, claiming and rejoicing in wholeness through accountability.

Maybe it is because I put so much energy into taking time to fill my internal cup. Maybe it is because I have more financial freedom than ever before. By no means am I suggesting I could stop working and survive without income. I'm not at that point yet! I just have a deep understanding that the energy and the universe I work in conjunction with are so in tune with my needs that they will find a way to manifest and provide them for me. I also know that I still need to put out the effort and work to manifest these needs, and I just do not spend time anymore on stress or worry over the money it takes to maintain my whole state of health. When I hear so many people saying, "It is what it is," I want to scratch my head and say, "Yes, it is what it is, but do you want to accept that fact without even the slightest inclination to change it?"

Small moments of total awareness, showered and sprinkled with a twinkle of kindness, teach and remind people that we are all born from and will all return to the same connected existence. I simply know that when I look someone in the eye and say, "You have a nice day," I am making that connection personal for them. I think that small example is so imperative in setting examples of awareness, bringing back personal validation and creating loving forms of action.

I will use the example of salt and pepper. Alone, they are a single seasoning, but combined, they are what we commonly call a combination seasoning. They make a great "team." One amplifies the other, together creating a taste, balancing a perfect blending. In sync, my body and soul commit to working together. I have become friends with my ego and accepted that my ego has every right to be living in my body. My ego is constantly reminding me I am in human form and I make mistakes, judgments, comments that really need to be addressed on a personal level. In this union of body and soul, I claim those lessons, making them personal. With this wisdom, I am quicker to react and know my lessons in every experience I have. Claiming and accepting this without expectations clears my head and my heart to be available for daily interaction in every experience, without judgment.

Life choices are free and they are mine to claim. If I choose to rule from my ego, I will respond with frustration, anger, tears, strong words of injustice, or sadness. All these emotions supply tools offering a format for processing. If I respond with my soul's intelligence, I will have a knowing that supersedes these emotions. I will respond with an aged wisdom without emotion, claiming the lesson that pertains to me personally and how I should react to the lesson from ego.

This is the exciting part: you get to choose any and all experiences! You also get to rise above and not repeat certain painful lessons if you choose differently. You see, the awareness is in the humbling act of choosing. I could not have gained the knowledge if I did not receive the lesson. I have found a way to make friends with my ego, and we have a good friendship. The growth allows me to attain gifts for both my body and spirit, combining both worlds.

This combined education then graces me with wisdom to advise any situation that may present itself. I am armed and available for anyone asking for guidance or direction. It also allows me to be nothing more, or nothing less, than a mediator receiving channeled energy from divinely anointed to divinely asking.

The coolest fact is, the more you grow in love and light, the less threatening the world around you becomes. This is a true statement. The more you accept your entirety, your fragments, the more you cement your foundation. The more you cement living in the moment, the less worry you have about the things around you that you cannot control. Yes, I agree this takes commitment, acknowledgment, and a decision to buy 100 percent into this mindful practice. This way of thinking, feeling, loving, and living is all about firstly, your level of awareness and secondly, your level of commitment.

To say that these moments of enlightenment and miracles have healed me several lifetimes over would be a huge understatement. I get to witness many miracles that do not belong to me. But make no mistake, when there is a healing happening in, around, or through you by divine intervention, it heals you as well. An authentic light worker does not do this work to be healed or gain power or prestige, gratitude or status. This is just what one does when called to work with and for God. He/She/Source is the creator; you are the hands, voice, source to extend a channel of love and life. There is no other job like it! You get to still play in the sand and you get to work in the leaves all at the same time, accepting your human flaws and working with The Divine's perfection and existence, spreading unconditional love.

Cup Full Of Flavour

I am excited about this chapter. This chapter reminds me that I can have anything and everything I wish for at any given moment in time if I choose to experience the events that present themselves in my life.

Think about this: if you were in the biggest candy store in the entire world, how would all those colours, choices, flavours, distract you from picking just one? Would you simply not want to try them all? Some, you would want to have more of, deeming them favorites. Others, you would take a bite out of and put back. When I was little my mom would get those assorted bell- shaped candies at Christmas. Some of you may remember them; some may not, but these were hard, cream-filled candies with a very thin coating of dark chocolate. I would take a tiny, discrete bite out of the bottom until I found all the pink ones, putting the other ones back carefully in the box. My choice, although mischievously delicious at the time, always came around to my mom's scolding me for doing what I did to get the ones I liked the most.

This candy store from The Divine works the same way. If you choose a lesson, you may not be particularly fond of hearing the truth. In that event, swallow your choice and learn the lesson and do not pick and choose the ones that may be the easiest or may have the best taste. The result? Lessons, good and bad, teach you what you do want. More importantly, however, they teach you what you *do not* want to repeat.

This is what I have come to know with my overflowing cup. I can have as many choices and flavours as I wish, or I can pick the same kind of candy every time, as much as I want; the source is unlimited, allowing me time to choose. It is also without guilt, judgment, conditions, and calories! Sometimes, we can bite off a bit more than we can chew as we want to make bigger changes. Those big changes seem to take a longer time to process and digest.

Not all interactions or moments in my day leave a sweet taste; some experiences can leave a salty taste like tears. I am fortunate, or some might say not so fortunate, to be a place for people to share and feel comfort. Being an empath does have its challenges, as well as its rewards. The definition of "empath" is "a person who feels what others feel and experience." It has taken me some time to recognize and identify if an experience is mine or if it actually belongs to another person. Simply put, when people to whom I am connected cry, I also cry. Sometimes, it is a trigger related to a similar painful experience. Some actions are less than kind and can leave a bitter taste in my mouth. Resentment, acts of injustice, or less-than-kind actions that cause me to feel or experience the moment are something I call "tasting the flavours of my cup."

There are times when the pain people are carrying is bigger than their bodies are capable of handling. This may cause anxiety and fear to leak out around them. Empaths can feel these toxins. Empaths join in celebrational energy as well news of a new birth or unexpected windfall. Tears come to clients in sessions of healing and releasing old scar tissue from present or past lives. Often when this healing occurs, we shed tears together in a combined healing. One of my favourite things to say to a client in tears and healing is, "When you heal, the world around us heals. I also receive the healing." I have grown accustomed to the salty taste my tears bring and welcome with gratitude the healing on all levels. Healing can be accomplished by things that still surprise us and can happen most often when you don't expect it, allowing you to just be open and receptive to all the moments brought to the experience.

There are times when I get a bad taste in my mouth and regret deeply the damage my tongue has caused by my actions of speaking before I gave enough insightful thought to my words. This bad taste has also happened when I chose selfishly an action that may not have been either morally or legally acceptable by society's standards. Or I may have been judgmental or misled by my own ignorance of something I have not fully understood.

My calling is to listen, be open, and validate the request. Next, I accept the responsibility to channel from Divine Source and deliver the gift to the one asking. I have also come to understand through this type of interaction that the person asking always receives the gift. Taking responsibility for their own need is a prerequisite for the gift or multitude of gifts they will be receiving. Again, and this is key, I am just the facilitator and the channel for the gifts of wisdom and enlightenment this person is requesting. I get to channel these precious gifts and requests from The Divine directly to your life source. Your own healer within receives these gifts in your personal 'Innerspace'.

Be kind to your healer within. Pay attention to the hunger of your own self. All hunger pains require different sources of food, supplying your vessel. Pay attention; spend some valuable time investigating your personal needs. Make lists on paper or create a sacred space in your soul's heart. Keep track of your growth. Record it. You have unlimited space inside to reflect your best interests. Don't be afraid to ask yourself personal, pertinent, painful questions. It is the only way you're going to learn who you really are and what your body, mind, soul are craving. More importantly, what types of food do you require to feed, nourish, heal yourself? Sometimes, it is literally food like protein; maybe you are dehydrated; sometimes it is books of knowledge, meditation, drumming, yoga, or walking in nature. These are all food or prana for body and soul.

Pulling Weeds From Your Cup

I am sure you have all had a few weeds you wish to purge or get rid of, causing you to stop, ponder, and then choose a solution that may be more productive for you. I have had to weed my own inner garden, picking out stones and debris on several occasions. Some weeds can be deceiving; they may even look pretty, like they might belong to the garden, sporting a nice flower or pretty, green foliage. However, soon you might discover the true nature of the weed. It may grow so big that it starts to suffocate the garden, blocking the sun, depleting or limiting food source. These weeds can be deceiving and subtlety destructive, and they tend to grow quicker than the rest of your garden.

I want to share with you a weedy patch of my garden that had accumulated over a time span of two years before I was able to identify it, get down on my knees in my garden, and pull it out. Over a decade ago, I worked with a man and found that being in his presence was often personally upsetting. I felt powerless around this strong, forceful personality. I struggled for over two years, trying to identify my emotions of anger and frustration around this person. It is not that I did not like him; what confused me was I did enjoy his company. I admired, even marveled, at the way he could carry on a conversation and hold his own, and the way he conducted his daily business quickly and efficiently. What I realized was that the way he treated women in general always got under my skin. I personally witnessed this on several occasions. It was subtle, but it was real to me because I, of course, took it personally. One day, as I was watching him verbally stroke a customer into submission, it dawned on me. It was like I had a huge lightbulb moment. The switch went on! You know those moments when the heavens open and the choir sings out? I knew in an instant what had always bothered me, and this provided the spark of knowledge I was seeking.

The following morning, I approached him and asked if I could have a word with him privately. I sat down across from him with sweaty palms and took a breath. I looked him in the eye and said, "I want to thank you." He looked at me, confused, and asked why. I proceeded to tell him this: "For some time now, there have been things about you I haven't liked. There have been times I have felt you have personally disrespected me in a subtle, dismissive way, and this made me feel uneasy. I have felt angry towards you over the years for the injustice I claimed personally. But yesterday, it dawned on me why it was so personal for me. Those very same characteristics in you, the way you use and manipulate, the way you seem to control, are the very same characteristics I don't like within myself. I saw in you the same things I have witnessed in my own actions, in getting what I want or what I need from people. This awareness touched my heart yesterday, and I realize I really don't want to live this way. I thank you for teaching me through your actions, what I need to do to change my behavior towards you and others. You have been a very good teacher for me. Thank you again for listening. This will help me to accept you for who you are, and not take you so personally." He did not say one word in response. I thanked him again and left his office, not really knowing what the outcome would be.

How did this end? It was very awkward between us for the next few weeks, as we defined new boundaries. We did not instantly heal and gain respect for each other. The truth is we never talked about the subject again. We did, however, become closer in that we gained a mutual, kind respect for each other. The new boundaries were established and adhered to, respecting the truth we gained about each other. To this day, if I run into this person, we give each other a big hug and we know exactly where we stand. Was this a weed in my cup? I would concur with my ego and soul: it was, indeed, a weed in my cup, but here is the moment of clarity. It was my weed; mine to identify, address, and confront. I had to see what kind of weed was growing in my cup, understand its origin, and have the strength to address it and pull it out. What is left is a space, a hole. I get to choose whether to plant new life, new trees or new flowers in my cup. I get to plant my future dreams and desires, filling that hole. How powerful, how exciting, creating new life within my own internal garden!

Weeds come in all shapes, forms, and sizes. Weeds can be substances or people; they can be habits or addictions; and after pulling them, they can grow back. Have you ever noticed when you pull weeds how fast they grow back, sometimes appearing overnight? Spending some time in reflection, identifying your weeds, can allow you to pull them daily if you need to. Weeds may reappear when you least expect them to, by hurt inflicted or unexpected bad news. Life happens every day, and if you want to gain some control in your cup, instead of dreading the pulling of weeds, perhaps calmly accept that they are just going to grow. Be ready with your spade and your bag of rich planting soil, digging up your weeds, replanting, filling the hole.

Accepting and claiming your new garden can be very gratifying, healing, and calming. This process can be like internal strength training, regaining power and forming new commitment. This can help build self-esteem, also allowing you to set some new, healthy boundaries. You get to choose; you get to gain back your personal control by cultivating new growth in your own internal garden.

Weeds can be destructive and, if not addressed or taken care of, weeds can take over your whole internal garden. Yes, we are still talking about the garden within you - the garden you get to design, create, and transform into your masterpiece; the garden that you build, created by your own design. This garden, if you choose to section it off into stages, allows you to plan, taking your time to build your desires. You are the designated gardener of your own garden. It is your responsibility to keep the weeds out. You get to tear down and rebuild anytime you want to make changes. There have been periods of time when I have had separate little weed patches, especially if I am working on a rather stubborn habit. There are periods of time in my life where I am pulling weeds for several weeks to clean and clear my cup, and still the weeds continue to grow back. The results after cultivating my garden: a period of dormant sadness mixed with exhausted bliss, waiting in wonder as my garden heals and grows, sprouting beautiful new life. It is exciting, rewarding, tiring, inspirational, and taxing: all healthy and all needed stages to enjoy all the fruits of the time and labour you invest in your garden.

This information may stir up internal mud causing murky water, awakening emotions that have been lying dormant for several years, or even lifetimes. If you suddenly become aware that you are walking around in a daze of despair or feeling a deep-seated sense of loneliness, it could very well be that you have some unresolved issues, buried heartache, or loss of self-respect causing emotional pain. These splintered fragments of self can cause bruising on, as well as deep within, your heart. You may have little or no conscious memory supporting these feelings. I do know if you are not happy inside yourself that it is up to you to find ways to fill that internal space. I am referring to your internal cup.

I offer this information fully for each of you willing to change your life. I would share anything with you that you might require from my own cup to start you on this quest. You never have to be alone; you only need to sincerely be open to asking for what you are seeking. Again, if you could choose from my cup, what would you choose?

How To Keep the 'Fluck' Out Of Your Cup

(Disclaimer: My editor told me I couldn't use the word 'fluck' since it is not really a word, and we did not want to use the actual word I am intending here so as not to offend my readers. I'm sure you get the picture, though. This is just another one of many "Tracey-isms!")

While still freshly on the subject of weeding your cup, I asked myself why I would not share with you my daily struggle of how to keep things real. It is not easy working as a light worker. We are often called Healers - people who choose to work in and with The Divine Source. We are labelled, like so many others in life. It is not that simple and it is not that complicated either. My father says it best when he calls me an 'idiot savant'! And in calling me that, by no means is he insulting me. It is just my father's sick sense of humour poking fun at his firstborn child. I was administering Reiki and blowing violet breaths on his toe one summer, drawing some of the infection and swelling and trying to relieve the throbbing and pain, when he said, "Tracey, how does this work and why does this work?" My simple answer was, "Dad, I don't ask questions. I just do what I know I am called to do every time The Divine Source presents a need." I know this to be the way and the truth from my inside out.

I will try to explain the title of this chapter the best way I can. I am human; I laugh, talk, and live highly on my emotional connection to all living things every day. I buy into being a human, fully experiencing the grace, fun, excitement, hurts, pain, and disappointments, like all of us living side by side and sharing space on this planet. It is unrealistic to think life will go along without conflict, personal judgment, injustice, or actions I do not support or agree with. So, when I say "how to keep the fluck out of my cup," 'fluck' is the closest—made-up—word I can use to describe what I really intended to say!

I often use this word spelled an entirely different way, accepting that sometimes it is the only real word that makes everything okay depending on my emotional state. I use that word in many different forms of expression: frustration, elation, anger, injustice, shock! It feels good to scream that word out, or whisper that word very softly like you are saying it under your breath. It is a non-denominational, universal word. All languages understand it. Try not to take yourself too seriously when you use it yourself, but note that saying it can be a great, instantaneous, free stress reliever.

I have stopped trying to be superhuman. I have stopped trying to shove my belief system down people's throats, thinking that my way is the best way and the only way. I just live in my fullness, my richness, my honesty, fully aware of my flaws. I am real and I am grateful! I make mistakes every day. I lose my temper. I swear like I mean business. I throw my head back and laugh from my belly often in my day, sometimes more than once. What saddens me is that I believe it to be true for a vast number of people with whom I connect, that they need to sacrifice and compromise a part of themselves to be saved. They feel the need to rise above their true nature of being human, denying the right to live life fully and embrace the life they were born into, experiencing all aspects. They believe they need to sacrifice and give up "living in fullness" to be a better person.

That, for me, is like amputation and delusion of your real self. It reminds me of a child being disciplined for a wrongdoing decided on and then punished by a peer or a parent, banished to their bedroom and not being able to play outside with childhood friends. This creates a sense of soul sickness. Parents feel the need to be so strict that they choose to stay in a stagnant state of existence instead of addressing other kinder options. Because I am so "soul sensitive," I feel for everyone in this state of existence. It is a familiar prison to me. I know because I have many times been imprisoned in those same lessons. Did those lessons serve me? They probably taught me to choose wiser in the experience or lesson even if it disappoints me. So, yes - it still teaches me through the disappointment; in other words, there is always a lesson, no matter the cost.

I know in my heart, though, the truth and this is so exciting: The Divine Source loves me entirely, complete with dysfunction and flaws. He accepts me when I fall from grace or when I live in grace. How exciting is it to know for me that I am fully accepted, respected unconditionally? It is life-saving! This awareness that I am loved in every state I choose continues to allow me my freedom of choice. This freedom allows me to be more creative, expecting less from others and more from myself. This existence makes me more accountable to change the things I can and to change the things within me that matter to my greater good - this whole being of mind, body, or soul state. This way of living allows me to have no limits on the endless possibilities, and I get to experience full life. Knowing this to be my truth allows me to be okay with exactly who I am every day. I know I do not have to choose only one way to live or that one way is the only way to enlightenment. I know I can still be human, eat hot fudge, be entertained, and visit places people might frown upon, and yet still be loved by The Divine. I also know that to stay in this light of love and grace, I need only one thing: unconditional loving kindness. When in this state of grace, you always make good choices. Have fun making choices! The results are the rewards you are entitled to receive.

I can be quite vulgar, boisterous, loud and sometimes very overwhelming. My personality does not always meld so well with others. I have flaws that are a little dusty and downright dirty. I am selfish and, at times, domineering. I have a deep need to be centre stage. I am so aware of this that I set intentions daily respecting personal boundaries and sharing oxygen with the people with whom I work and cohabitate. I know that these personality traits were born into me with the ego and body experience I chose this time. I know that not all people will fall in love with me. I will even go so far as to say some people will not like anything about me. I am totally okay with all this truth and, quite frankly, this is not about the 'fluck' in my cup. It is about the 'fluck' in their cup. I needed to embrace this and spend time honing, fine tuning, listening, understanding, and allowing myself to seek self-satisfaction and gratification. To say that you will have 'fluck' in your cup until the day you die is just being honest with you. Accepting and finding some comfort in this fact would be my hope, so that you can find some internal peace. This loving, internal self-acceptance will grant you courage and give you what it takes to work on loving others with the same zest and honesty with which you have come to love your full self.

Choosing complete honesty with who you really are can leave you raw and vulnerable, but also as strong as titanium. You need to be brave and you need to be strong. Some people may see this as a threat when you present yourself in this unblinking revelation of your truth. There are times in your growth that you struggle with good and bad or have ups and downs. In these cases, it may seem easier to shift the focus or blame or judgment. However, my growth and experience have been that when I am truthful, "awareness" follows quickly after acceptance. This key word unlocks the hidden knowledge in your moments of experience. When you accept, your fate is sealed; you are choosing the experience itself, and that lesson becomes your truth.

Keeping the 'fluck' out of my cup has been a constant, lifelong personal challenge. Sometimes, I even use that word to shock people into talking or releasing, using laughter, pointing out the lighter side of healing. Humour and belly laughs can bring about more healing than you will ever know. Try it and you will be pleasantly surprised and might even seek it out. I think our transitional spirit state is pure bliss, including laughter. I cannot stress enough that we are loved in our entirety and fullness, without judgment. We are guided, and we are cherished, and we have personal guardian angels designated to protect us and share and teach us from the moment we take our first breath.

We are loved and we are never judged. If you really think about it, we are the ones who do all the judging, choosing, deciding. SO - I say, embrace the fluck out of your cup. Find your joy! It is what teaches you. Joy is the ingredient I most often use when I want to leave a mark on a heart, and this mark often makes a difference. Laugh at yourself! Be kind to yourself! Have fun with the child who never grows old; this child who lives inside of you; this child who has a home in your heart, connected with your spirit, conjunctively living this great magic carpet ride of ups and downs along with you. Stop and just give yourself a big hug and say, "What the fluck?" It is another beautiful moment I get to spend making a difference! I believe we need to get busy living fully in the moments that opportunity presents.

Not that the "I don't give a fluck" attitude can't rear its very ugly head - it can! But seizing the moments and living them to the maximum can be very exhilarating and therapeutic. Sometimes, I straight up say to people, "There ain't no U-Haul behind a hearse!" And that is the flucking absolute fact. We cannot take one thing but our naked bodies and attached souls when we leave this life. One of my very personal mottos - and I really do try my very best – is:

To live in love and fullness!

Cup Stability

I was fortunate enough to have had the companionship of wise women on our drive to and from work the year before I retired. These women are funny, strong, and sources of deep conversation, laughter, and comradeship. I often had a healing on the rides to work and back home, sharing conversations and debating. These women are good sounding boards and have given me ideas and lessons to write about. This chapter comes from a conversation I wish to share with you that took place on one of those eventful drives home.

I had shared some of the chapters of my first book, <u>Innerspace</u>, and we were discussing how they came about and the fact that we have experienced the meaning of life, full circle. We all seemed to be in similar stages in our home lives, and we started reflecting. Not by any means were we comparing, but just sitting back and, in our own awareness, talking about this subject.

We talked quite a bit together about how blessed we were in our lives, with our families, and the truth that the foundation in our cups was stability. In the awareness in our conversation, we realized together exactly how powerful being stable in your core is and how it impacts and affects your entirety, in all your choices and the outcomes that follow.

We discussed how we could sit back and be aware of other people around us struggling for that same security we realized we had; this stability that is cemented in our core, providing healthy balance. We collectively realized that although we experience different lessons, we often end up in the same healthy space together. This space, we described as "peaceful awareness." We realized that the time spent together on our drives home provided us a safe haven to discuss, sort out, and compare notes. It allowed us to be aware of what we could be and whom we could support. It allowed us to love deeply, caring and sharing in kindness. It allowed us to laugh until we cried and cry until we laughed. Our friendship has endured and is cemented by a common denominator: stability in our cups, teaching us to be aware of the moments that matter, moments we share with each other.

What never ceased to amaze us in conversation was that we agreed to identify without judgment how others were getting stuck, providing the three of us with a deeper understanding of the situation. It allowed us to understand others on a level where we felt safe and taught us the deeper meaning of compassion. This knowledge was gifted to our hearts and souls, giving new perspective on understanding other people who may have shared their experiences and helping us to understand that it was not about us, so we were not so deeply imbedded in the lesson of the person sharing it. Without the emotional attachment, we could then be supportive ambassadors, warriors, weapons of love and hope for others as they travelled through their lessons; teaching us, if we chose to combine experience collectively, that we could all share and grow together with a sense of purpose and light in the understanding. These lessons allowed us to be present, choosing to be open in the sacredness of sharing. We, as living beings, can then trust and grow together with the wise wisdom of divine presence.

We know we are blessed with the gift of trust. This gift keeps us aware and allows us to remain open if we are chosen to listen and support someone who has the courage to share their struggles. We are aware that it is an honour to be asked to provide support in their time of need.

What happens when you are chosen?
- You know you are blessed.
- You know you need to listen intently and not judge.
- You know you will then be a vessel of love, hope, and direction.
- You are a channel of divine love and healing that pours out and into the person who chose you.

- You know you will open your heart and soul and, with intention, ask for words of kindness, truth, and love. You will ask for this love to rain down and saturate you with all the knowledge you need in the moments of the asking.
- You advise, listen, council, hold, wipe tears, hug deeply, and love unconditionally.
- You are available whenever the moment happens. When asked a question, think with your heart before saying no to aid the wounded person seeking assistance. Be fully present.

The Divine knows how much we can handle, how much the world needs, and what He desires all His children to have. So, the key point is: TRUST with all your heart and soul, with a knowing that you will be all you were intended to be, with the support of the universe backing you. You will be given answers backed up with miracles and validation daily. All you need to do is say "YES!" and accept that your life will change. We are blessed! It is our birthright to accept these blessings and become anointed daily with a divine love that knows you so personally, He can count how many hairs you have on your head. The Divine was with you at conception and will bring you home and carry you into spirit when you transition back home.

In the meantime, enjoy creating your stability, building your security, securing your cup foundation, making it strong and pliable. Fill your cup with any colours you desire: bright pink, deep orange, soft meditation yellow, or beautiful, deep red clay! Create it, build it, mold it, sustain it, become it! Stability in your cup will make you wise and secure and strong enough to build anything you wish to support and create inside your cup. In this process of strength building, you will be able to batten down the hatches and survive through any storms that may come your way. Trust that you have faith; that you are able to create a strong foundation. Trust what you love about you, and allow yourself to make the constructive changes you need to rise above and beyond the fog. This clarity will show you how to sustain the truth into which you were born. This truth will teach how to live your life to fullness.

Cup Full Of Fear

Fear is real. It can stop us in mid-action or thought the moment it surfaces in us. Fear stunts our growth, petrifies and immobilizes us. Fear gives us a reason to stay frozen when things become overwhelming and we need a physical time-out. Some people think fear is a nemesis. On the other hand, fear can be a very useful tool to have in your cup.

Fear can be incredibly productive if you embrace and accept it. The emotion of fear typically provides us with warning signs that can appear in several circumstances. I will try to give some examples of my experience with this emotion.

When I was little girl, I had a particularly hard time understanding boundaries. And I still do! It is something I continue work on daily, defining that fine line. I crossed the line often as a child, disrespecting my parents who were just trying to parent, teaching me lessons. Sometimes, in what I can only say must have been frustration and poor communication, they would lash out and I would become fearful. The anticipation of the spanking I was going to receive when my father came home instilled such fear in me that I would feel stimulated to the point I thought I was going to wet my pants. To further the intensity of the fear instilled by my parents, I would have to wait long hours of uncertainty in my bedroom, conjuring up the most horrific torture that would be inflicted on my person. I can tell you in all honesty, it was never as bad as what I dreamed it to be. I think the threats were always worse than the punishments. And then I would hear it: the sound of my father's steps coming down the hallway to my bedroom. Fear is real and can cause so much dysfunction later in life, as it surfaces time and time again as a result of certain triggers caused by insecurity, neglect, and abuse.

Fear is a real emotion, one not to be taken lightly. Fear should be treated with kindness, compassion, understanding, and discernment. I still face my fears daily, directly or indirectly, sometimes bringing me to that familiar state of survival mode. Fear invokes real emotions of frustration, anger, passion, all real and raw. Fear drives my cup; it ignites my cup, causing fractures; and fear keeps me frozen, causing anxiety. These fears cause confusion and delusion, clouding perception and direction. Fear can be contagious. It can spread like a wild fire and claim multiple victims. This emotion is real and can paralyze you in a constant state of full-on survival mode. It has no mercy and can gain power as it escalates into a series of both physical and mental repercussions.

Fear is not the end of one's life, although there have been times when I felt my life was ending due to fear and lack of direction. Knowing what you need to do in a situation that creates fear is powerful. It may be that a particular drama you are claiming personally is the root cause of the pain you are experiencing. In this case, I would suggest you literally step out of your situation if possible. I say "literally" because taking a physical step back provides a space to wrap your head logically around the situation. This step back gives your soul a chance to converse with your ego. Stepping out, allowing a time-out, may make you feel uneasy as this is an unfamiliar solution to addressing fear. It may even seem strange at first. This stepping back might make you feel like you are walking away when you should be standing ground, fighting for your worth, especially if the fear is coming from a confrontation with another person. However, it is the only honest way you are going to have a clearer, more decisive plan of action that is built on love, reflection, acceptance, understanding, and kindness towards oneself.

Stepping away could be as simple as physically taking a step backwards, putting your hands on your heart, calling out loud or silently asking for the aid of any saint or archangel, even your guardian angel. They are by your side in all ways, always. They are directed by The Divine to not interfere unless you call them to aid you. Truly, they come and you have an instant shield of protection surrounding and supporting you. Honestly, I promise - if you call, they will deliver, aid, love, and guide you. They are gifts for you. You belong to the angels and the guides around you. Their mission is to protect, love, and aid you at all cost! But remember: **You have to ask for assistance!** Practice this; ask them several times a day to show up, to send you signs of love, compassionate words of wisdom, visual signs, spontaneous signs. Be aware that they are sending them to you. Buy into this reality fully and be open to receive. Look for them connecting with you. They were made to love and support you, as you were made to love and support them. It is a two-way street: we need angels as much as they need us. We are called to be love and share love between each other.

Breathe in all your gifts of divine support. Share these gifts with the world around you. They were given to and for you so that your fear may dissipate and subside. These gifts will help you regain ground and live in full harmony, living life with less fear and more passion to learn the lessons you were called to learn, loving the masses you were called to love.

Do not let fear stop you. Do not let fear control the beautiful light being you were born into. Try to find that balance, that thin line of balance, that allows you to understand the emotion we call fear. This emotion known as fear was given to us to be used as an aid in helping us to discover our wholeness in the healthiest way. It was not given to us as an emotion to overpower our well-being, but as a tool to teach us and an emotional gift to protect us. This may sound very strange, but I believe it is the truth. If you think about some of the times and situations you have been in when you have been fearful, the fear itself causes you to react in a way that might help you save yourself - emotionally, physically, and spiritually.

The more you become aware of yourself, your state of mind, your physical health, and your spiritual growth, the more you will recognize how fear affects you personally and how to be directly accountable for the lesson. The results? Claim these lessons that provide tools to extinguish the fear around the situation. Always going directly to spirit or Divine Source softens the blows and the amplified physical pain fear can inflict. Allowing connection with this source leaves you feeling less hollow. Divine Source fills up your bone marrow, saturating your being in loving energy, warming, comforting, and validating your existence. This connection of conscious energy essence enters your body, fills you, and exits through the crown on the top of your head. You may feel the effects of this divine energy physically, with warmth and tingles all over your body. This spiritual life force collectively gathers legions of spiritual light workers who are quick to jump in to soothe you, bringing forth a message of such magnitude it can only be described as an all-encompassing, magical connection. This life force and wisdom know what you need in the exact moments you need them. You only have to do one thing to receive all these gifts of grace: "ASK FOR THEM!"

Reflections In My Cup

Reflection often, for me, is a time of quiet contemplation while meditating. Reflection, if you are open to receiving, can happen in any given state. Awareness is always the result of my reflection, living out my scenarios and lessons from my daily choices. Reflection happens in the moment you wake to consciousness and encourages you as the momentum of living continues throughout your day. You get to set the tone; you get to make the choices on how you play out your day. Reflecting is imperative to building core balance and is the perfect tool to teach you stability. Reflecting on gratitude sets the tone to provide a humbled state of peace.

When you were a child, did you ever have an opportunity to lie on your belly looking into a very still body of water, where the water was so crystal clear it looked back at you and you saw your own beautiful face, eyes, smiling back at your reflection? I can still feel the warmth of the sun on my back and see the smile of contentment at the stillness of the water. I could see the depth underneath, life moving, floating, swimming, plant life swaying to the current underneath the surface of the water. There was life existing completely in a world of its own. This life carries on, sustaining itself, oblivious to your watching from above the still surface. I wonder if The Divine ever sees us in the same manner, watching us from a place of serenity, smiling a huge universal smile of love, sending light.

I remember how fascinating this experience was and I could lie for moments, sometime endless hours, watching the world move and sway in a place that did not even know I existed. My special spot was a very big irrigation pond we called "Chisses," right smack dab in the middle of three huge tobacco farms less than a quarter of a mile down our road. It was a place that was off limits to me according to my very strict mom. I was never to venture there, but something pulled me like a magnet to cross that unforbidden territory, and the temptation was too great, making the threat of punishment for disobeying seem insignificant and worthy of the outcome if the secret ever got out.

I often relate the story above in the same way I feel and experience the spiritual energy of The Divine. The great energy connection is much like the physical child in me when I was little, lying on my belly gazing into the water. The universe is looking at me in the same way, gazing at me lovingly, watching the life force grow, change, move on inside of me. There are so many changes going on under the skin, deep within my soul: new growth, new life, shedding seasons, changing colour.

I know for me as a child, if I did not disturb the surface, I felt special. My place was sacred. It was like I was privileged, engaged, somehow a part of this world, bearing witness to the life unfolding in front of me. I could feel deeply that bearing witness to this world was a gift and a deeper, life-long lesson from which to learn. Back in those days, our mothers would send us all outside with lunch and some Kool-Aid, trusting we would obey all the rules of the house. But what does a child do when rules are made? Oftentimes, they look for ways to sidestep and challenge the laws that were mandated by their guardians. I can talk about this now because, firstly, I am no longer in fear of spankings, and secondly, forbidden fruit always tastes that much better. Let me tell you, when my mother was wagging her finger and implementing her rules, she meant business! Trust me! For a feisty, almost-five-foot person, she could instill the fear of The Divine herself!

These memories still leave me awestruck: to know that there was another world going on in full living moments, unbeknownst to me. It also gave me a bigger insight for my future. At the age of eight, you have no idea what 'future' even means until you look back and reflect on the subtle miracles that were setting you up to become the person you were intended to be, which brings me back to reflections.

Spending time, even just a few moments a day, in reflection can be a very productive teaching tool. Reflection teaches discipline and structure in the core of your cup, this special space inside your body where your soul resides, functions, and joins your flesh body. I have a designated home for my soul, and since being introduced to the chakras in my body, I have gained the knowledge of their existence in my soul field. I see my soul settling into its spiritual house inside my physical body. My soul lives mostly in my Kundalini chakra, which is located right at the bottom of my spine. In that space, if I put my hands back and align them, I feel a small, hollowed-out triangle section between bone and flesh and that is the space where my soul rests. I know to you this may seem a little hard to comprehend: that a soul would take up residence in a space as it is in spirit form and, as far as I know, is not always bound to my body. I am absolutely positive that, for years, my soul takes a time-out, a sabbatical, and leaves its home, my body, and travels in the astral field, everywhere it wants to be, go, and experience.

In daydreaming, meditating, or dreaming while asleep, I have come to know and understand that these states all lead me to reflection or a state of contemplation. This state has always been a productive, active tool that advances my thought, then the action of delivering my truth, addressing it honestly and kindly to the masses of people who involve me in their existence. This interaction connects us, allowing us to experience healing and growth together while sharing. How incredible is this chain reaction in the truest form? Wholeness!

I know, without a doubt, there exists a universal life-force that loves us and desires a connection with us. It is as real as the reflection in that pond so long ago, smiling back at my own reflection. The universe sees me the same way. I knew instinctively that if I even breathed on the water, it would change, scare off and disrupt the living organisms underneath the rice-paper-thin surface. However, I could watch it move and live and choose its existence and its way of living and witness the miracle of life I was not a part of, yet connected to. How awesome that this same life force watches us in the same way, being careful not to intrude or change our paths unless we acknowledge and reflect on the help and guidance we seek and then ask for assistance. How respectful of this universal, loving, wise energy to not change our course of action, but to be ready to assist if we just reach up with our hand on our heart and ask it.

Reflecting in my cup has taken time, effort, and energy to form this habitual routine. Reflection has allowed me a time-out to think things through before reacting with an emotional outburst. Reflection has a different effect for me than meditation. I do enjoy meditation, as well, because I can slip away to a place of peace and calm by repeating a gentle mantra or just breathing, allowing my body the privilege of slipping into a state of grace and constant peace. It is more like gently sweeping thoughts out of my ego head space with a soft feather duster, or sometimes a straw broom. Reflection requires thought and action. It is done quietly, and it is specific. Reflection teaches me patience on a whole different level. Reflection advises and helps me understand what belongs to me to claim as my personal choice of action, as well as quickly showing me what does not belong to me. Reflecting continues to help me claim personal accountability. It educates me in the moment so that my actions of love and peace demonstrate the true moments in which I am living. Reflecting in my cup has become a very valuable tool to aid me in attaining wisdom to be a kinder person, present in mind and soul. This kinder person teaches me to take life a bit less seriously, which allows me to lighten up and become less intense, bringing my cup to fuller joy and ultimate happiness. Is this not what we all seek: Creating a desire to keep a full cup?

Cup Strategies

I think, for me, this chapter rings true with the education I constantly receive from the healers and light workers with whom I am in contact. These committed, often humble, quiet workers choose to live in a peaceful state of physical simplicity, and quiet, methodical, private mind and soul space.

For some of these workers, I am quite sure I presented a challenge when first getting to know me. My oftentimes unconventional presentation - how I think and work - may be a bit overwhelming. Because of my boundary issues and my seemingly endless barrage of questions, I might be a little exhausting for advanced mentors. Most of these workers are well beyond my years of knowledge and hands-on experience and are often amused by my naïve sense of not even knowing I am intruding. These workers seem to already know what my questions are going to be even before my endless queries. I have so many varied interests on a subject matter or methods of healing or working with and in conjunction, sharing our gathered gems of information, that I must be to these gurus like a grade two student loaded with caffeine. But I just can't seem to stifle my exuberance. I just know this is how we grow and share our wealth.

There have been a few workers who have been assigned to me and I to them, given to each other to further teach and share collectively our methods of healing and power. The older and wiser healers, light workers assigned to me, have been patient, teaching me different strategies and methods to use when meeting and working with clients or potential clients. In the past year, I have grown considerably by doing nothing ordinary and expecting extraordinary intervention. I will try to explain my methods.

In the past, I have preached about letting go of expectations and holding on to acceptance. This commitment to action has become my most cherished asset in the past six months. For a long time now, I have been helping clients in session cut cords of past scar tissue and redundant pain and memories to clear a path and space, in a soul sense, as well as physical body. This process of cutting and clearing out allows the client to continue on their journey with less pain and more room to make a new and powerful, healthy existence. I am so committed to this healing method and, time and time again, I witness new life and healing.

I do not think I ever took on the challenge on a conscious level. As of late, every day I recommit to saying out loud, "Let go of any expectations and accept all things that come into consciousness for you today. Tracey, be completely open and full of heart to receive and to digest. Tracey, expect nothing from any situation or relationship to which you are committed and emotionally attached. Let go of any attachment, unkind or uncaring comment or judgment you may have on the subject matter. Wrap your arms around the situation, embracing and accepting it for what and who and why it is. What matters is to love and not to judge." Some days, I am very successful with my intentions; other days, I have to forgive my angry outbursts of emotion and judgment before I go off to sleep at night.

This new, internal shifting and not committing personally to any situation allows me the freedom to see, hear, and be a better source of love and light for the actual moment that is happening connected to my being. Now, you may be thinking you would have to be dead or nominated to sainthood to be able to pull off this loving action all day long. Truly a myth! Truly not so! You can choose this action every time by not reacting and not expecting, but through the simple act of acceptance and, most importantly, instant forgiveness.

In this instance of acceptance, what happens is remarkable. In less than one second you switch mindset. You simply see more clearly what it is you are accepting, instead of expecting any kind of reaction or action. You claim your truth and let the rest of the expectation go. It's quite simple: it is not yours to hold on to. You get to witness the choice. As previously noted, the result of this action is pure, unadulterated freedom, and when you incorporate this in your daily practice, you begin to live in a constant state of peace and clear awareness.

This has also started to seep into my worst habit: the wondrous world of food and my body's craving for instant gratification. Unfortunately, I still struggle with my 35-year-old eating disorder. The truth is when I do overindulge, instead of being embarrassed or flogging myself for my addiction to food, I embrace and accept the flaws of this disorder. In doing so, I can forgive myself and resolve to make healthier choices. In the past, I have had many people talk to me, teach me, advise me on this subject. I have achieved great results with some strategies and not so great results with others. In the end, I am grateful for the knowledge I have gained, but it is still my acceptance of the disorder and not having expectations of myself that helps me deal with my addiction to food. It is only through this acceptance that I have the grace to forgive myself and move on to the next moments I have to live.

When one starts to truly see the lessons learned, which often require repeating before they are fully grasped, the result can be exhausting, both physically and mentally. On a soul level you know the truth, and on an ego level you fight the truth. It is like the ego wants and needs to be fed these lessons or addictions to sustain its life and validate its existence. For me, this cup strategy helps me realize that all the lessons I was repeating were simply exhausting my energy level tri-dimensionally. This has cleared a path for me of acceptance and made the rest of my life lessons easier to understand and quicker to get through. It also has allowed me to understand that others around me are there to help, or not help, if I choose to ask for support. It is comforting to know that things are meant for me to finally grasp on my own, but lifelines are always available.

These new strategies are helpful for me to quickly identify and claim what I need to claim. Strategies do not have to be complicated. For me, they are a productive plan, a communication tool, law and order for my next moment of awareness. Strategies hold me personally accountable for my actions and my direction, for my focus and my existence. Strategies create a plan; they deal with the past, clearing space and making room for a presence in my future. Clear, precise direction can act like an internal and external compass. Strategies encourage growth and stop repetition of old patterns of destruction or scar tissue; comfortable, redundant patterns of lessons already received.

I have come to embrace my world totally and completely. I have a full understanding of the meaning of the word "gratitude." I encourage everyone to have a plan, and to fight for the existence of pure gratitude, living fully in the incredible gift of life into which we are all born.

A Second Cup

This chapter is dedicated to second - or third - or fourth - chances to keep your cup overflowing with abundance. In a world that mandates perfection and decreased face-to-face communication as a result of our increased reliance on technology, we can, at times, become disconnected in a sense. Who in this century is not guilty of lashing out with your fingers on a computer, cell phone, or Facebook page? Who in this technical world, if not born into it, gets somewhat confused with abbreviations and the lingo of the cyber-world?

I would like to see us still incorporate some old school logic and consideration, communicating personally as well as making use of this new technology that has taken the world by storm, allowing room for both forms of communication. I, personally, have witnessed the way the younger generations, and even many adults, have become attached to the technology of choice on a never-ending, 24-hour cycle. While initially causing me discomfort, once I chose to embrace our modern society and accept people and the way they choose to communicate, something magical happened. I stopped expecting them to act in a manner I thought or deemed to be proper behaviour. I stopped expecting society to embrace the rules I was raised under and started to look at the changes in the world around me. This does not mean I enabled or accepted bad manners or behaviour; it just means I started to understand the way the majority, it seems, are communicating and to accept this method of choice. Once I allowed myself to actually accept this way of communication, I no longer judged others for their choice.

This reality, this new method of communicating, became less of a personal attack as I also tweaked my own interpretations or assumptions that this form of communication was disrespecting me. It became less about me and more about the way this generation communicates with each other. The tools provided are just different skills, in the end with the same results: We are still communicating.

I put myself in the place of the multitude of youth I witness living this way and wonder how much this constant communication, consistently being plugged in and connected like this, would consume my identity! This lesson was so subliminal, yet so hard to resist. I ask myself how it would feel for them to not commit to the easy access and impersonal connection these devices offer. This thought not so long ago would make me feel sadness; yet, my new awareness lets me understand that the sadness comes from me and relates to my old world dying and the new world arising. I know I must find another pathway to shed light into this new millennium, providing a new method for individuals to hear the message of self-worth. How? By simply accepting that we can and will make a difference by remaining open for new ways, consistently spreading love and providing a comfort zone.

I have witnessed the younger generation sleep while eating. I witness them going through life existing on autopilot. They are connected and plugged into a technical life force that is all-consuming. We, as parents and teachers, witness short-circuits and overloads. I think we have all come to realize the plus side of technological advancements. Our youth today seem refined, educated, and quicker to solve problems in group settings. This technology has some very valid uses. It teaches us that the world is more accessible and has a great deal to offer, making it possible to attain our goals. Education is a powerful tool.

The part that I have a harder time dealing with on a personal level is the decrease in face-to-face communication. For me, that lack of physical and emotional connection leaves marks on my heart. I miss the connections of tears of joy or sadness shared while communicating intimately with each other. That kind of communication has been fading away with this universal, instant connection at your fingertips. You can speak out through technology and get an instant response. You can feel it, but not experience the human bond of intimacy, and this, for me, is missing the element of human touch that brings it all home.

I have found that empathy, accountability, acceptance, and forgiveness seem to be taking a backseat. Going back to old school values, these attributes and our commitment to them were our driving force, our tools to communicate our needs and desires and truths. These qualities taught us respect and personal accountability. If you did not have these attributes, you did not have the means to attain success or the ability to live life fully. I know that if I do not accept all the changes, I will not be able to shed my light for anyone in need. I get to keep all my tools in my toolbox, however, as someone may ask for assistance and I intend to be fully prepared to be that torch of wisdom!

Second, third, and even fourth cups are new opportunities for me to gain acceptance and understanding. It is difficult some days to not judge a generation that does not speak my language. I struggle often with patience and the comprehension to fully embrace and accept change. It is what my parents expressed to me time and time again: The Generation Gap. I am truly experiencing the Generation Gap, where I find myself more frustrated and judgmental instead of trying to accept and embrace this way of living. In my daily mantra, "Stop expecting. Start accepting," it makes it easier to let go of the false sense of control I have and to embrace all in love and light. I will continue to work on accepting this social media world. I need to use the tools and gifts it has to offer. These gifts allow me to continue to spread a message of love that I believe in completely and am passionate about. In the way our children talk with their fingers, sharing this cyber-world with their own kind, I will be sharing my message as well. We all can work together: same message, different means of communicating.

I believe if I stop expecting and start embracing, I can be accepting of this normal way of communication for our youth, and this may open doors, supporting a means of communication between both generations. This open-mindfulness may present an opportunity for our youth to have a peek and consider incorporating some of the older generation's belief systems. I have gained this knowledge and so may my future lineage. Maybe this open-ended acceptance of each other will encourage us to try out some of the old ways in conjunction with some of the new ways. If the seed is planted with good intention, they may consider mixing it up, sharing the well of knowledge, encompassing and combining options and methods. All of this can be accomplished by simply allowing room for all of us to love and accept without conflict, criticism, or judgment. This will require huge amounts of patience and tolerance; it will require open minds, souls, and hearts. There is no room for ego in this delicate dance of old versus new life. If we all are to get along and respect each other, we need to teach what has not been taught in this generation: tolerance for slow, methodical consideration; respecting each other; and then the true meaning of patience.

So, I say enjoy fully the flavour and the satisfaction of tasting slowly, savouring the second, third, and endless cups of experience it takes to create your own way of living and loving. In this world, find a way to communicate love to our younger generations, expanding their horizons and dreaming their dreams. Your dreams are just as imperative and important, and they add so much richness to the endless cups we are yet to experience.

Friendships In Your Cup

The beautiful thing about friendship - and it is remarkable - is that you can have different kinds of friendships. Friends are not like family designated by life blood; friends are chosen by you. Some friends are lifelong companions who grow with you, intertwined like vines in and out of your life for the whole of your existence. With childhood friends, you cherish and reminisce when you meet up over special holidays, celebrations of birth or death. Soul friends are those with whom you create deep bonds and spend time socializing and supporting each other in life's good times and bad.

Friendship is so important! It sustains us and validates our worth, providing rich, deep history spanning decades. Friendship unites our souls and fills our cups, encouraging and supporting us. We have all kinds of variety in our friendships: some grow with us; some outgrow us or we outgrow them. In some friendships, we find we have short sabbatical seasons with them; they are teachers brought to us to help us gain knowledge through life lessons, forming the relationship that develops between us. You will learn eventually how to accept all connections, developing a full understanding of the vast difference of what friendships mean and what they deliver. Friendships fill your cup, and your cup will continue to flow and flourish through the connected state of friendships.

I have very few relationships that I can say I have intimately, personally committed to on a friendship level. I have many people who live in my heart, to whom I am devoted and regularly send love and healing light. Friendships, however, are different for me. I allow few people into that space for a few reasons I will share with you.

I am selfish with my time. I am committed to working with the masses of the people who experience something intimate every time they ask a question. I have no more room or need for anything more personal than my work, and my being has its guard up if anyone shows the slightest interest in becoming more than a client or an acquaintance. This attitude can backfire on occasion. We choose our connections for specific reasons: to gain acceptance or validation, to feel safe, to learn lessons. There are people who have gained access to my heart and slid inside it, claiming a bigger piece of me. This lesson of letting them in has been a huge gift of understanding what it means to receive as much as I give out.

This kind of friendship is required in my life to help me learn to share and receive, as well as to teach me to say no. When I do say no, I am just being honest and, with love and kindness, I explain my answer, which is usually to establish boundaries. These relationships teach me how it feels to be loved without conditions, freely, with understanding, attaining complete acceptance and learning the value of giving to others. These types of commitments make us take a time-out of our own lives, making room for other people who need something from us. Even more important to note, these people have a need to give something to us so they feel validated. This kind of friendship can create a new birth inside us that we never realized was there and teach us how to share our wealth, teach us to be less selfish, or sometimes to be more selfish when helping us find our truth.

I have been blessed over the years with different blends and levels of friendships. I have sustained a few lifelong friendships. I have gathered seasonal friends; we share and teach each other, gaining mutual respect and admiration in the experience. I have learned the true meaning of reason friend, season friend, and lifetime friend!

I would have to say in all honesty that I have more acquaintances than life-sustaining friendships. I used to feel obligated to sustain these friendships and that it was my responsibility to touch base, keep in touch, and check in. Anyone who is living in these times knows the pace and demands of life are increasing and many people do not have the kind of time necessary to continually check in. We have been warned over the years that the world is spinning and shifting and speeding up. The expectations that the world puts on individuals to be accountable is not a realistic request. For me, I am present and committed to being aware in my presence. In those moments of living life full on, I work towards maintaining my own accountability. In those moments, I can focus and be committed to living life. It is my pledge to myself and also to my fellow man.

Living this way has given me a new perspective on the complexity it takes to encompass friendship on all levels. I have become more responsible to my personal commitment and less responsible for filling a void in the person who has befriended me, or the expectations I put on myself to fill my own void through this friendship. That is not what friendship is about for me. For me, friendship is unconditional, honest, refreshing, life sustaining, and most of all, freeing!

Miracles In Your Cup

Around the time I completely committed to the practice of not expecting and started accepting everything coming into my life, something truly started to change. I would get up in the morning and commit to the idea of expecting miracles in all shapes and sizes, and I got to see the actions playing out before me, witnessing the manifestations. From the moment I woke up, I would say, "Bring on the miracle, the healing moments. Please teach me to be conscious of the miracles that are manifesting."

I have taken the liberty of sharing with you some memorable happenings in the messages I received. Sometimes, there are many more than just one moment of magic that happen throughout the course of a day. I have the privilege of witnessing miracles with other people in my life, which enhances the validation of the miracle. Together we can converse, and while connected to the spirit the miracle happens all over again in the power of three. There will be manifestations of love and light spreading out and illuminating the dark corners of the world with the powerful actions of love and kindness.

In my previous employment, we had a department in our head office that worked in conjunction with the employee store next door to the office. This allowed the flow of B-B (business to business), and staff would often leave passes in the reception area for various groups to pick up so they could shop in the store next door. On one occasion, a retired firefighter arrived to pick up some passes. He had very bright blue eyes and a strong British accent. I took a moment to listen to his interesting stories of 35 years as a volunteer firefighter.

After he finished sharing some snippets of his life, I thanked him for his service. He became quiet, thanked me for asking, and paused, almost as an afterthought, and said, "You know, the most emotional experience I ever had was the time I was chosen to go to work with the New York firefighters when 9/11 happened." He proceeded to tell me he carried dead bodies out of those buildings for five weeks. His eyes filled with tears as he told me that was a time in his life that still leaves him humbled. Thanking him again with tears in my own eyes, I was left in a state of awe and numbness for the sacrifices he made. I was humbled, blessed, and touched deeply and stayed in this state for a few minutes, praying that God would send this 'gentle man' graces in abundance for his loving act of kindness. I was filled with awe and gratitude that I was privy to his story and his message of unconditional love for humanity.

On another occasion, a woman came in to the office and we chatted for a few minutes regarding her questions. I had barely noticed the stroller she came in with or the five-month-old baby inside it. As I sat in my chair answering her questions, I felt like something bigger than I understood was pulling me out of my chair and dragging me over to the stroller. It was literally a pull from my soul to the baby's soul. As I made my way over to the stroller, I was starstruck by this young child. Her mother was present beside us, but that baby's eyes and my eyes locked in a spiritual dance and soul embrace so intense, I could not peel my eyes away from her ancient, incredible soul. Her mother was in awe as we continued to embrace, and I gently told her she was here to help us save the world and make it a loving place of kindness. I could not help but utter out loud, "Here you are and we are so much richer for your choosing this timing of re-entry with such a joy-filled, loving, spirit of hope." This child was so intense, it brought tears of joy to my eyes. She smiled only once and I smiled back, her gift leaving with me a fragment of her huge spirit. I tucked this miracle moment into my heart for a long silence after the mother and her child carried on with their day. I know she has a secret of healing to share with others. I know our divine universe will continue sending these kinds of messengers, sending hope, educating us. These light workers, I believe, are here to teach that eventually we will come to understand the power of unconditional love. Accepting and acknowledging their existence brings their message of truth, even if it is delivered by one tiny baby touching one soul at a time.

On another occasion, a lady came in with an issue to be resolved. After listening to her and offering two possible solutions, she started to relax and share her story - a sad one. She had lost her mother the previous year, at the age of 58, to a very sudden heart attack. She felt safe enough to share and so started to speak freely about how difficult her year had been. She continued to talk about things her mother used to do for her, supporting her own growing family; how her mother would take care of her daughter and her grandchildren, cooking and sewing and caretaking. She started to feel the emotions she had been holding on to and let go, trusting that she could express them to a stranger, and I supported her in this release. She then stated that she also had lost her sister, as well as her niece, and she released again. At this point, I did tell her lovingly that I work with universal energy and life force, and I shared with her what I have witnessed after we leave our bodies. I further explained a bit of my history of being present in these transitionings. I proceeded to tell her that her sister had a message for her, and she agreed to hear it. Her sister then told me that when she left her body, their mother was waiting in spirit and they both waited for her niece to join them. This lady was open to hearing with her heart and soul as she listened to the words of love being expressed from her family members. I assured her that her mother, sister, and niece were constantly around her, helping her breathe and feel calmer about daily life. I came around the counter and held her and hugged her hard. I then blew two violet breaths: one breath on her heart, another on her third eye chakra. I continued to hold her as I said, "Your family loves you through me. Hang on to this moment and know it is truly happening." We did not speak, but we experienced that moment of something bigger than the two of us happening. I then came back around my desk, looked her in the eyes, and said: "Sometimes, things are bigger than words." She thanked me and as she was leaving, she turned and said she needed what had happened and the experience had made her day. Well, that certainly made my day! Yes, I know they are coming: miracles. I witness them every day, in many moments, shapes, signs, and happenings. I even have grown to recognize them in my sleep.

God sent yet another earth angel to me recently, and we have exchanged quite a few words and thoughts together; she, feeling safe enough to share her life with me, seeking to gain spiritual knowledge. She tells me often that she writes down what I say and goes back to reference the interaction. When you connect with someone seeking growth, firstly, it is a gift; you were chosen. Secondly, it is a responsibility. You must be open to The Divine, to listen before you advise, always remembering that they chose to work with you and confide in you. In their awareness of their needs and wants, they come to a full understanding that they do not have to make these difficult choices alone.

Through this support, they come to understand they are connected to a vast greatness supporting them as they make healthier choices. In communication with another enlightened person, they too are enlightened, confirming their truth soul to soul. They then start to be open to the word "synergy." Synergy means: "an interaction or cooperation of two or more organizations, substances, or other agents to produce a combined effect greater than the sum of their separate effects." *(Concise Oxford English Dictionary)* She told me, validating this truth, that the times when she shares with me and is struggling the most seem to be the times I am prompted by Spirit to send loving reinforcement her way.

This action brings me to healing tears in bearing witness to the growth spurt we have witnessed in her. I cannot tell you how proud I am of her courage to heal; so proud of this brave woman who embraced her fears. She glows with happiness and happy thoughts. She stands stronger than ever on her convictions to claim happiness no matter the cost. Watching someone climb out of Pandora's Box, open her beautiful wings, and, with grace and love, spread them out wide and fly is like watching a miracle of love unfold in front of your own eyes. In this moment, you get to experience with her a rare and personal occurrence; you are privy to her new birth. Did she have to die before she could be reborn? Absolutely! Was it painful and frustrating and fearful? Absolutely! Can she fit back in that box again? Not even one part of her fits.

I want to share an interesting fact: after two years of not being in the same space together, we still receive powerful messages from the soul connection we shared together. We get a message so strong in our hearts that we reach out with a text message. It seems mostly the magic between us is a repeated number or sequence of numbers. These powerful numbers have a personal message to and for us. We know without one doubt that we receive these gifts of validation and connected love from God's ambassadors watching over us.

I love this person mostly for her kind and beautiful, untainted heart and soul. She has kindness at the core of her every intention. Will she have bad days? Definitely! We are all human and ride the roller coaster of life at every turn, sometimes with white knuckles and ashen skin, and some days with our arms up in the air screaming, bursting with exhilarating adrenalin. She will continue to build her life, and it will continue to unfold as she sets her course. I will always be here for her if she needs me. She said something to me that made my jaw drop and, with her permission, I would like to share it. She said, "Tracey, you know when…your friend said you were glowing at the wedding? I meant to tell you that she is right. I noticed it a while ago… it really is like a light. I can't explain it. It is something I feel when I think of you or I am near you, or you are talking to me…The best way I can describe it is like, if hope were a person… hope would be you."

These interactions are the divine gems you gather, giving you the memories to keep your cup sated and happy. You now have the knowledge to reference these moments, words, heart drops you have tucked away in your cup. You get to take them out anytime and revisit them. This keeps your cup full of life, hope, and the reality that miracles do exist.

Miracles are everywhere! The sooner you accept these unexpected gifts, delivered constantly to us in our every waking conscious moment and dream state, the quicker you will come to recognize them. They can be minutely small, and yet so incredibly earth-shatteringly powerful. If you are not paying attention you might miss them; they will just gently pass you by and travel to the next available person seeking them. It has been my experience in bearing witness to miracles, that I receive the most joy in the small moments. The bigger miracles make me hold my breath. I can literally hear my heart beating in my chest when the big ones appear. The smaller ones just seem to seep into my heart space, collecting, gathering, accumulating, resonating personally, feeding and encouraging my growing connection to all life. I recognize in these precious moments that there has been a connected presence of living communication from both worlds. To be privy to the miracle, no matter what it manifests, is the mystery of the miracle itself. I expect I will not know how or why until I am fully in spirit form, once again, returning home. The Divine sends and the miracle is received, and, in that instant, a universal action binds our essence together. Miracles create validation, truth, experience, memories to be stored away to remind us that we are loved and cared for on the days we need them most. Time and time again, this happens: you open and say yes; they come; and you see with new wisdom bubbling up from the vast canyon of your eternal soul within.

Music In Your Cup

There is something in the air at Christmas that makes it magical. People are nicer in general, warmer, more inviting, and kind. They seem to talk and share more personally. It just seems to be the way the season unfolds. On one particular day, the line-up in the drive-through where I get my morning coffee had seven cars in a row paying it forward, covering the cost of the orders of people behind them. I know this because I, too, chose to do that for the driver behind me, and I was car number seven. I only hope kindness continued with the same loving intention. It seems that the general public smiles more, engages more reflectively in kindness towards strangers, and responds lovingly to the people close to them. I guess that is why I try to keep this season alive in my heart every day, trying not to let anything extinguish this light known as Christmas spirit. I am sure you are no stranger to the question, "Are you ready for Christmas?" I always have the same answer when asked this question: "Christ lives in my heart every day, so I am always ready for Christmas!"

Here is a Christmas miracle I had the experience of receiving one year and wish to share with you. A woman came into our store wanting to exchange some boots for her child. She was stunningly beautiful, and after we exchanged greetings, we were able to get her sorted out and new boots ordered. We started to exchange words and stories and she started to glow from inside her soul, becoming angelic in the conversation we continued to share.

We talked about her father and her daughter and her gifts of the spirit. I came to understand that her son, then 10, was born gifted and when he was very young, he started to tell her about people who had passed on. He would share details about them and tell her that Jesus would come and bring them to the light. I sat and listened to her tell me all these wonderful things and confirmed them in my own heart. I felt her gifts and her son's gifts as truth, confirming the same things we both cherished in this knowing. We were both brought to tears several times during this conversation, in awe and rejoicing that we were given these special moments to share. It was always so anointing to me that during these "God breaks" at my job, the phone did not ring, and other customers did not walk in. Every single time there was a spiritual lesson or an interconnection with His earth angels, this would happen.

We continued to share our lives and talked about the book she was going to be writing, the book I had just finished writing, and other ideas we were considering. Then, she told me she was a professional singer and for years sang on cruise ships and in musicals. She had retired to have her family and was currently working as a talent scout for child singers all over Canada. She was fascinating to listen to, open and full of white light and love. The way she spoke for God and her bold acclamations of love and light were incredible.

It was then that I asked her if we could please sing a song together, and she said yes. I moved around the counter and felt instantly like I was going to be saturated in a gift of Divine Spirit from head to toe. She then said she was reading something about Joy to the World that morning, so I suggested we sing it. It was like we both opened our mouths at the same exact time; the music just poured out of us. I sang the melody and her beautiful, powerful voice threaded like a velvet cord with harmony, matching it note for note. It was perfect; like a symphony from heaven. People upstairs left their desks to come and listen and were left speechless. The music our voices were creating lifted us to the celestial plains. When we finished singing, we just looked at each other with glistening, moist eyes. She spoke first and said, "God has gifted you with the gift of voice and music." She told me I was powerfully anointed and should use my voice more often. She also proclaimed that there was an angel standing behind me with a bow and arrow, and that when I sing, the angel shoots an arrow; my voice lands on the prisms;

the arrow pierces into peoples darkened hearts; and my voice then lights up their hearts, clearing the darkness. I have always known my powerful voice mends and heals broken people. It had just never been told to me this way.

I had watched my mailman transfixed all week, as the week before Christmas I sang him a Christmas song of his choice daily when he delivered the mail. He would just soak it all up and walk out and continue his day, with a smile on his heart and new fire of love in his eyes for his fellow man.

Never, ever, underestimate the power of The Divine using us all when we commit to saying yes in whatever way suits us best. When you say yes, you become an ambassador for the greater cause. This yes teaches you the meaning of sharing, delivering a universal message of love and hope. This is achieved through simple action or combined interaction, with the aid of the universe working through and with you, uniting us all. This choice is not a threat to your unique individuality; it only adds peace to your existence and an all-knowing to your destiny.

A Peruvian Cup Of Tea

Recently, my partner and I had an opportunity to experience Peru and all the beauty that South America has to offer. Lima was never discussed as a travel destination by Joe and me, but Joe does enjoy South America, so when the opportunity to visit Lima presented itself, we said, "We're in!" The "what if" factor always allows me to be open to the next experience presenting itself, and in this case, it graced me with a cultural education I was thrilled to embrace. I will try to share with you in words what Peru taught me and the riches I gathered there.

Joe and I traveled with great friends with whom we have spent time on a regular basis over the past couple of years, and who truly love what Lima has offered them over the years. When this couple talk about Peru, it is obvious to anyone willing to listen how much they have fallen in love with the place. In reflecting on our times together, we realized that our friendship has grown and continues to cultivate new growth. This continues to fill our cups, bringing us joy. We realized that we do not need to be friends; rather, we want to be friends. The desire comes from four strong, successful, creative beings finding joy and connections. These connections stem from the truth that we grow and learn from each other. The joy comes from the connections we share in the journeys we take together. We know we are blessed with this divine connection we choose to continue to cultivate. We, the four of us, have equal gifts to lavish upon the friendship table where we share our experiences.

I was sitting back reflecting, possibly after a pisco sour, Peru's potent national drink, and I had one of those moments - the kind where the heavens open up and you have an epiphany. It was a distinct moment, one I can recall right down to the time of day and the food on our plates. Joe was happily chatting, and I was intently listening. He was smiling, and there it was! In that moment, I understood our connection: we all have an equal amount to offer. As simple as that, there was a moment of understanding the freedom and ease of our relationship that continue to feed us as couples and as friends. In that moment of friendship, I recognized total freedom. No one wants anything extra. We simply enjoy giving and sharing in the moments we have together, without keeping score or having agendas or expectations.

What seems so much fun and continues to bring us all joy, in my perspective, is acceptance, in the core meaning of the word. In other words, we are all separate, different, unique personalities, yet we all resonate in our souls. We are learning a totally new level of communication because we accept what each of us brings to the table. As a combined consciousness, we listen and we grow together. Most people spend an entirety not being heard. This is a true statement, so I will repeat it again so that the statement sinks into your being: Most people spend their entire lives not being heard! Digest this sentence! The friendship we have with this couple has taken us on a truer journey of self-awareness. The common denominators in this group of friends are love and kindness. It was a great moment for me to sit back in quiet reflection after enjoying a traditional Peruvian dinner of mouth-watering beef and delectable seafood. While contemplating the dynamics of our friendship, I understood true acceptance of and by each other. I am so grateful for that awareness, teaching me by grasping an understanding that there is always room in your cup for healthy relationships.

During our time in this South American city, we ate at the finest establishments, as well as the local native hot spots. What remained the same in every moment of our experience was gratitude, respect, cultivated honesty, and quiet grace. This living grace seemed to radiate from the Peruvian people. Life in Lima is slow paced, and the city is surprisingly not overly crowded considering its size. In fact, the population forms a contiguous urban area that consists of almost ten million people. The peaceful essence of their beloved homeland seemed to be sewn into their DNA. It resonated in their spirits. Their dedication to their culture and the respect they seem to have for their Christian roots is firmly and proudly planted in the earth, clay, and sea around them. It was felt in a peace that seemed to saturate and permeate the actual landscape and was alive in the air. It was like a unified movement of people with a kind essence, awareness, and happiness that generated from within them in spirit. That is what I felt everywhere we went, with every gesture of respect: the gift of kindness.

Some might suggest that this calm, peaceful spirit comes about because the weather is constant, with just the perfect amount of sunshine every day. You wake up and 360 out of 365 days of the year are a repeat of the day before. You experience sunshine, moderate temperatures, and the same easy, comfortable existence with no harsh elements to contend with. The weather could add some merit to the theory of peace and the calming effects that dominate the energy in Peru, but I happen to think it may be deeper than that. People still have a choice every day: to choose happiness. Claiming responsibility for the way you live your life always comes down to choice.

I could talk about our personal experience and how the four of us covered literally over 51 miles of the beautiful city of Mira Flores, which is part of the metropolitan area of Lima, and our experience of how the wealthy and the working class live. I could talk about the bartering at the Blue Market and the energy that was exchanged in that space; so many vendors crammed together, so jam-packed, trying to make a living, surviving by selling the same things the next stall was selling. It was interesting how people were drawn to each other, using different forms of communication, trying to get you to purchase from them. Some made connections of attraction; some made you feel like deflecting and avoidance. I could talk about the beauty of the Alpaca Market, and how my partner more than once, in an artistic bouquet of hand-made love, felt like unleashing all the llamas and setting them free in the mountains. I could talk about the walks on the top of the huge embankment that stretched for miles and miles, capturing the beautiful, powerful sights and sounds of the ocean crashing its waves upon stones. The sound, if you stop and close your eyes, brings you in seconds into a trance, with the subliminal power of the trance bringing you quickly to a state of awe.

I could talk about the reverence the Peruvian culture has for God, the crosses of Jesus, the sacred day they hold as a national holiday called the Immaculate Conception of Mary. The native people of Peru celebrate with street parades and committed followers. In the churches and the catacombs buried beneath the Cathedral, the sacredness of times gone by oozes from the walls, filling my heart and soul with a deep, rich longing to have known a glimpse of the Saints they honour. I was humbled to have walked into a church while High Mass was being delivered around me in Spanish. People were on their knees on slabs of cement, praying with their rosaries, offering up decades of personal prayer.

In my quest on this trip I wanted to find a church where I could light a candle to honour the people who had asked me to pray for them. Of course, when I set out an intention, I am on fire until it happens. None of the churches I ventured into for the first few days had any candles to light. Nowadays, many churches have converted to coin-operated candle boxes that are electrical: after the coin is dropped, the candle lights up. This does not actually have the same effect, but nonetheless, the intention was there and the offering up was completed. So, as it happened, we did stumble upon a church and off to the side of course, there was a place like I have described to you. It was a bit more private and as I was seeking a candle, I found one that was unlit, so you can imagine my sheer joy. Unfortunately, I could not for the life of me get the wick to light. A kind lady came over and started speaking to me in Spanish and tried to help me. At the same time, angelic music started to pour out of the speakers. I truly thought I was having a descending angelic, divine moment. This is the funny part: Yes, this woman helping me was an angel. She took the time to help a stranger by teaching me a trick to the lighting. She was a master at it; she took that worn-down candle and succeeded in lighting it from another one that was lit. She saved me from burning my entire fingers off! With gratitude and with tears in my eyes, I hugged her as I had a lump in my throat and could not speak words. Joe came up and stood beside me and whispered in my ear that he had put some money into a box and music began filling the church. So, I am happy to say I encountered two angels that day: Joe and the lady who helped me deliver on my promise to everyone for whom I said I would light a candle, sending prayers up on their behalf!

One last thing I would like to leave you with on Peru, although the effects will live on for me for years to come. I was standing in the street watching a parade of hundreds of people holding up and carrying a sculpture of Mary, in celebration of the Immaculate Conception of Mary Day. I was in awe at the following that seemed to have more purposes than order. Joe suggested that I ask one of the priests if I could take a picture of the procession. Anyone who knows me knows you don't have to say something twice and I am on my way to seek it out. I walked over to the very congested street of people. I got the attention of one of the younger priests, made a gesture of clicking my fingers in the shape of a camera and proceeded to ask through my body language for a photo. In a matter of seconds, there was a scurry of fast Spanish, and in quick order it seemed as if a swarm of men, at least eight to ten, had surrounded me like a huge angel wing on each side. There seemed to be a leader they gathered up like a High Priest and they put him in place to the right side of me. Then with some other kind of order, the rest of the group put themselves in place around me. I felt a pressure of love that was so huge and reverent, and it was a holy moment in time. People stopped and took photos. Joe also took some. It happened in the blink of an eye and lasted maybe a minute in total, yet the effect was profound as I floated back to Joe with eyes streaming tears, and this feeling stayed with me the entire night. The priests all handed me cards of their famous Patron Saint, and they were all speaking to me in Spanish with urgency to heed the prayers of the sacred cards they were giving me as gifts of love. I took the cards and clutched them to my chest in gratitude. I have since given them out, dispersing them to people who I know will be blessed by the gesture; they have a deep, pure faith and spiritual love. Overwhelming spiritual gifts are always there to be received when you ask for them. This was just a reminder for me to ask often and receive the gifts from a divine love that wants to shower me. In my growing, I can then share the wealth for others to receive gifts from my overflowing cup of gratitude.

One of the most magical places we visited on this trip was Parque de la Reserva, one of the largest water parks in the world. The four of us headed out together on a quest to see this beautiful park. It took us several hours to locate the park, but when we did find it, it was beyond fabulous! The fountains kept flowing, changing, filling as we sat together, snuggled up on a wooden bench, starstruck, taking in the wonders, colours, pictures, and textures. Just for fun, close your eyes…catch your breath slowing down, feeling it steadily, methodically becoming one with you…and imagine a waterfall filled with explosive colour shooting up from the ground. Attach this thought to your soul. Let the vision fill your cup with exquisite Peruvian tea, and experience the joy of feeling satisfied and refreshed.

Our lives are forever changing. People in perpetual soul motion and who are like-minded get to have great experiences of awareness. These experiences nourish and educate us. I am aware, now more than ever, that we all have our own personal journeys. Thank you for sharing this cup of tea with me. I enjoyed talking to you about Peru and how the magic of this trip kept filling my cup.

Cup Full Of Shepherds

On one occasion, I was deep into a conversation with an enlightened co-worker who had worked very hard on gaining ground in her perception and experience, processing and validating her journey. I am inspired by her brilliance and the gifts she so generously shared around our work table. She is smart, but not just smart - she is intelligent; bold in her true acclamations. She is so refreshing! I have watched this passionate, compassionate woman grow, planting seeds for people to ponder and grow from. She has been able to excel in her position and her personal life; she is an excellent boss, co-worker, and wife. I do love her, and when we have the opportunity to share stories, common denominators in our truth, it is like a fire starts in me. We feed each other in conversations, sharing growth and supporting each other.

This lady held a very responsible position requiring many tentacles, working with many different kinds of people. She had come to find new tools of communication, giving her different options as to how to get what she needed to do her job. These insights allowed her to be firm and forthright, sprinkled with kindness and bold humour.

One particular morning, we talked and shared some things we had both been processing independently. After she left my desk, I realized that what we had shared was pertinent to my personal lesson on that day. She was my first face-to-face miracle of the day. I realized that we were getting the same valuable message of not expecting and just accepting our designation and our choices. I realized that she, too, saw definite value in having the awareness of the meaning of 'choice', and in the act of choosing, adjusting and accepting the lesson, paying it forward, moving on. She and I concur that the world is full of sheep, and although they are sweet and kind, they are often led astray by a pack of wolves or a sly dog aiding the pack.

Sheep need shepherds. Shepherds need sheep. Shepherds are designated from Divine Source. It is a calling. I believe a shepherd is a designated person who leads. Sheep are people learning to become shepherds. I believe some people reincarnate even more than one lifetime before becoming shepherds. I believe earned wisdom through the experience of life as human is necessary to understand the challenges and the diligence it takes to become a shepherd. You need a desire that comes from deep within to be a vessel of love and kindness. This takes extreme patience to do your job, recognizing and receiving a message from The Divine. The message usually involves knowing who and what your next assignment is. Because your assignments are never the same, you need to listen carefully and know when you need to let go and move on. This will leave a path of love and light to show you the way.

Shepherds need to listen with their hearts and see with their intuitive gift of sight. Shepherds use all their human senses, as well as their cognizance, to do the job they are called to do. People who are called to this service know who they are and will talk freely to each other, recognizing that they are speaking directly to another shepherd. I know this to be true. I recognize who they are as light workers and co-workers. I know when I am in the presence of a shepherd. My cup fills in conversation. I am connecting with non-judgmental, truthful information that flows from facts, stimulated by a common denominator: internal, divine wisdom.

Talking with like-minded leaders brings you to a place of complete wholeness, with deep understanding. You are not working alone, although many shepherds are quite lonely and often isolated. When you get a chance to lay down your staff and join hands and hearts with a shepherd, your cup gushes to overflowing, your energy is rejuvenated, and you are enlightened. Your wick is trimmed and your torch re-lit, creating brighter light. So continues the process and journey you are on, with steadfast strength and love in your heart, leading your sheep. In this union with a fellow shepherd, you are reminded that there is bigger force at work, like a thick cloud of knowingness, connecting and threading you into one mission of loving action.

The mission a shepherd chooses is often lonely and misunderstood. A shepherd's actions may have a deep effect, causing ripples within the sheep's complacency or comfort zone. Shepherds can be quite vocal, often speaking with a direct tone of authority. A shepherd's strength comes from the strong hand of God. Shepherds act as agents, delivering divine, loving energy. Shepherds' work originates from a source of white light. This unlimited source supplies their knowledge, received from the highest power of all knowingness. If a shepherd ever advises you, if you are looking and seeking healing, closure, or divine wisdom, please heed the message they provide. All shepherds are on a mission, a calling of divine deliverance providing healing love. Please, try not to be offended if a shepherd leaves his or her mark on your heart. I encourage you to try and not take it as a personal attack. They are just providing useful tools to support or direct your steps. It is simply the mission to which they have been assigned on your behalf. They have received a message for you that may help you. Shepherds receive gifts of Divine direction, and because you have asked, they will deliver the message. There might be a struggle of the ego. There will be times when you will receive the message right between the eyes, and sometimes an actual kick in the backside. These are not intended to harm; rather, just to alarm or wake up the sheep seeking answers or closure. Healing is most always painful, but also imperative for new growth.

Do not be mistaken: the shepherd goes through something I call Soul School, or self-awareness training from Divine Source. As I have mentioned, every shepherd I know has been a sheep, repeating several lifetimes, gaining painful knowledge and experience. Shepherds have come to fully recognize empathy and have a complete understanding of patience. Shepherds experience pain and suffering and isolation through intense training programs, gathering an understanding of life and the repercussions of choices made through personal experiences. This teaches shepherds all the virtues and ultimate forgiveness of oneself and each other.

Sheep and shepherds need each other; combined, they heal together, understanding and aiding humanity, recognizing and practising love and respect, keeping each other humbled and grateful. They both have a job to do; one teaches the other. Please take heed and do not be fooled: sheep teach shepherds all the time in many different scenarios. It is important to know and understand this truth. These facts help to keep ego in check, working together to create a bond of unity. After all, our mission is one of sending pure love unconditionally; there is never any room for ego when it comes to these valuable life lessons.

Love life to the fullest. Embrace your sheep. Shepherd wisely. Take time out. Share around a campfire with another shepherd. Fill your cups; rejoice; find peace and comfort in the union of spiritual co-workers, and move on to the next fire. There is always room for more kindness, more cups of hot tea. There will always be another shepherd close by, diligently guiding and herding their sheep.

Cup Full of Soul School

I want to start this chapter off by stating that when I use the term "Soul School," I am speaking to you about something I have experienced on a personal level. It is my soul's experience in my human body. Over the past several years, all my lessons have collectively been growing and building a momentum, gathering information from a divine source of collective energy. This source, I label "Soul School." You know by now my way of writing involves describing my experiences using adjectives and metaphors. I have had several Soul School lessons in my life, and I have often used the words "Soul School" in referencing my experiences in my previous writings.

Soul School, for me, is an educational system of divine consciousness from which I learn. Ego learning comes from our world and the educational system we experience on this planet of varied subject matters, ethics, our curriculum. Designated education is truly important; however, I do love Dr. Wayne Dyer's take on ego, as I heard him explain in a presentation: Ego = Edging God Out. This resonates with me on a deeper level than ever before.

I talk a lot about being in love with Dr. Wayne Dyer. If you just spend five full minutes in this man's presence, he will tell you he did not always live in this state of grace. You can't help but feel a spiritual, authentic pull to this being. He, Dr. Wayne, is the real deal. He loves us all so deeply that you can absolutely feel his unending unconditional love seeping into your cup from every angle on your human body. He truly is present in the moment, and even in death he lives in the energy field around us. He loved us all too much to leave us entirely so my theory is he never left.

From the way time has been explained to me, linear time only exists for us in this world's dimension while we live out our lives in body on this planet. When our bodies expire, we transcend and enter the spirit world, another dimension. This world does not have the same linear time. In this world we see, feel, taste and experience life in this body. We make choices to learn many things. Dr. Dyer taught so many people so many things in his passionate life, and I know beyond knowing that he will never leave or forsake anyone who reaches out to him. I feel that he continues to carry on advocating for all of us in his spirit life. My understanding of life after death in channeling spirit is that if you remain open and simply ask, you can be with every connection you ever lost or loved. I am not sure if it even matters to spirit when they visit if the person they visit feels their presence. I believe that spirit understands all and has an awareness that surpasses ego. Most often while channeling, the spirit my client summons just wants to be near their loved ones, sometimes with a message, sometimes to simply connect.

Over time, getting to know Dr. Dyer through his works, I began to understand the pull, the common spiritual denominator, that law of attraction. He taught me many things through his mission of healing by examples of living and sharing. He taught me the value of spiritual intimacy that I claim to have with many clients before during and after session. This connection is not sexual or physical; it goes well beyond those emotions. It is a deeper knowing that we all belong together, joining as one mass of consciousness, combining one living energy. We are all seeking this connectedness; some consciously, others subconsciously. It is universal.

As I accepted and then adapted to the consistency and pattern of his messages, Dr. Dyer's genuine passion for all, a deep desire started to grow in me; a need to be fed and feed spirit to others seeking. I was saddened when it was his time to leave us, however, his bright spirit remains for all. His legacy, words, actions, and thoughts still manifest in the living, teaching us through his ever-present spirit.

I have become great friends with my ego. I respect it greatly as it sustains my life. It keeps my body healthy, teaching me to listen more accurately. This provides me ways to take care of the vessel in which my soul resides. Ego teaches me worldly, imperative survival skills. We need both educational systems so we can work together, learning from each other. When we share the wealth of both educational systems, we grow into one conscious mass of energy, on equal ground, coming together in unison.

My first experiences to justify this Soul School happened at a young age. I just knew about things I had no way of explaining, and most things I knew I did not share with anyone. I did not understand how I knew; I just did. There were times I could see things happening before they happened. It was never unnerving or scary, just my truth. This was normal for me. I always knew there was a God who loved me, and I could feel the support of angels, as well as masters and teachers, at a young age. As I grew into this way of living, life was normal. I just experienced so much from the true essence to which I felt connected that there was no way I could make it all up. It just became my truth, knowing of another existence, living in two worlds. My soul is old and has had so much experience. Be assured, if you also think or feel this way, there are more of you than you ever thought. It is okay to be okay, recognizing this loving source as it mingles with the world, walking by your side, enjoying the sharing of these life lessons with you.

I have never doubted that I have come from The Divine and will return to The Divine. It just is that simple for me to know I come from something much bigger. I am a part of the collective living energy that combusts inside my body, filling me with new love every day. If you choose from my cup, you can take whatever you need to nourish, feed, quench your thirst. I never worry if I will run out of anything; the continuous momentum of filling never stops.

People often ask me how, why, where all my exuberance and never-ending energy originate from. My answer has always been, "God."

It was harder as a child growing up to understand my life, my innocence, my lack of maturity. It was difficult to understand the source of life to which I felt connected and accepted and could feel only from inside me. But as I grew and the passion and the mission grew within me, I just came to befriend it and all collective sources of energy originating from God, and accepted all my teachers, guides, and scholars along the road.

I have had vast experiences in this system I call Soul School. How do I put this in words for you to understand this personal, educational journey? I guess I will start with grade system and try to compare it to our curriculum of worldly school and the educational system that most of you are familiar with.

When thinking back, maybe because I was so stuck and so unconventional in my grade school and high school classes, I believe I started my Soul School basics in my eleventh grade. I think it was in that time frame I understood I was clairvoyant, or another familiar paraphrase may be known as "third eye" gifts.

My spiritual awareness was planted firmer around that time in my life and I will elaborate on two incidents I had prior knowledge of before they came to be. One was a dark shadow experience of a boyfriend who passed away in an accident. I believe these occurrences catapulted my perception of living spirit existence. I experienced cognizance's opening through a door after his death. The opening I gained though a physical loss gave me spiritual gifts. Receiving these gifts gave me access to tap into communication on a spiritual plain after we leave our bodies. This experience, although excruciatingly painful, was an awakening spiritually. In the losing in body, gaining him in spirit allowed his essence to still live in and through me for many years. I know this truth, and am so grateful he loved me enough to hang out and hang in. We shared so many things and I am so grateful. This awakening brought me gifts I could not fully understand and scared me, maybe even stunting my growth for a while. I predicted things that happened, became reality, and kept most of these thoughts to myself. I could feel and see things that were real and visual for me, but not visible to others. This experience, if I were to try and describe it, was like I was seeing and feeling internally instead of the externally. I have always been able to see and feel from my heart center or chakras. At this time in my life, I had no idea the levels, layers, depth, or age of my soul; how it travelled, gaining knowledge in my sleep; or how it sustained a life force living inside this body I occupied. I grew to understand this life force, made friends with it, and accepted that the earned wisdom validated my existence on all levels of awareness.

Over the years, I came to understand my destiny to be more specific fine tuning of my soul, a calling. I could hear my soul louder than the voices I share in my daily life with my companions, co-workers, family members, and loved ones. Sometimes, I connect on a spiritual level with animals, as well. I simply hear them without vocal communication. It is like a living energy has grown up with me inside my body and has morphed into one being; a living, connected spirit mass of loving energy. I never question the truth that lives in the world of energy to which I am connected. It is always more of an afterthought in verifying with the person to whom the truth is being delivered from a lost loved one, or some sage advice I feel inside and need to pass on. It is in the validation of the person receiving the message that I have an afterthought or a moment of wonder in the miracle of deliverance.

Once you come to gain some sort of understanding of this connection, you will be guided through an intricate system of knowing on a deeper level of awareness. This awareness will guide you to your own self healings, messages, and life lessons, gaining insight and assisting others. Remember: You chose this calling and this journey of Soul School, working with the collective consciousness and divine energy. This living connection will assist you at every level of your learning, providing more tools and teachers in spirit, human, animal, and plant form; in all the elements we share space with on our magnificent planet. The learning and vastness of knowledge in these forms never end, and the educational system grows as you grow. You must forgive daily; you must claim your actions and reactions, which brings you very crisp reality or awareness. Just think: if you are going to be an ambassador for this loving wisdom of grace and kindness, the price for all these gifts is to share the collective wealth diligently, thereby keeping your cup full.

I once believed that because I did not do so well in our educational system of this world, it made me feel 'less than', limited. Not anymore! We are all blessed with unique gifts and offered many personal options to create and define our unique destinies, manifesting something we create and become proud of. It is so important to know inside that you are good enough; you matter; you make a difference just with your existence; you are a grand being of love and light, cultivating simplicity and greatness combined, living fully and proudly in confidence.

I like to say I graduated after receiving my Reiki Master degree from a university level of Soul School. It is where I learned to step out of ego and graciously step aside, giving the floor to my soul's attention. This open-mindedness humbled me; to know the truth of who I am and where I came from. This living energy source sometimes carried me, sometimes dragged me along kicking and screaming, repeating lesson after lesson of humiliation and resulting in deep, personal pain and human sacrifice. Without this dying and learning and shedding of layers, we cannot experience rebirth.

In the end, the knowledge and degrees account for just that: knowledge and degrees. They hang on a hook, collectively gathering dust if not used. Both worlds of education have valuable gifts to be used and spread and shared, so we can grow collectively in both the universe and the world, gaining respect and earned wisdom. It is our job to share the wealth, so it multiplies and cultivates new white light and a blanket of love connecting our living energies to one umbilical cord of collectiveness, sharing and teaching each other lessons.

I sometimes like to joke about being 93 percent air floating around in this body, living in the clouds and talking to spirits and spirit guides. Yes, I do feel them, literally, in temperature changes or tingles touching my hair. It feels like static electricity all around my head. Sometimes, I feel spirit hugging me, laughing with me, sharing experiences with me. I exist more often with spirit than I do as human on days when I have several clients booked. This non-judgmental spirit is kinder, and it is such a peaceful place to hang out. I feel comforted and loved, and these feelings bring me to tears of joy.

To say this is powerful is not accurate. It is so much more! To say this sustains me and gives me true hope for humanity would be more accurate. This universal existence does feed me and supports what I know is a true fact. For me, there is life after we die and there is rebirth. I know beyond all doubt that I will come back and recycle to learn more lessons. What we do not retain or learn in this lifetime, we come back and learn in another one. This thought encourages hope, knowing that, eventually, I will learn to incorporate all the virtues into practice quickly to recognize the magnitude of gifts they offer mankind. I love the human relationships I have as much as the soul relationships. They teach me how to be less selfish and how to communicate in difficult situations. They teach me how to share, break bread, and recognize flesh and blood. These relationships feed me, encourage me, and help me to understand compassion in a way that is human versus spirit. These relationships help me to grow with my ego, giving my ego a chance to experience life too. Human relationships teach me how to share my entire being.

I also firmly believe that not all life lessons we choose are going to be easy. Some of them will be beyond anything we can comprehend in spirit before we are born into the lesson. But I have come to ponder that if we cannot have the experience, how can we know the healing or forgiveness related to the experience? I am grateful for this life, this body, for my various deep and much-needed relationships. These relationships teach me compassion, patience, and kindness, through simple, daily, committed gestures of love and truth. I think I come back often to experience human contact. I love this life: the food, the cultures, kissing and hugging, eating exotic cuisine, and sampling excellent red wine. It is a privilege to have the use of both worlds and a privilege to travel between them, gathering information and truth.

From One Cup To Another

Where do we 'grow' from here? Imagine the endless possibilities! When awareness is heightened and you choose consciously to grow and heal, you have a conversation with your entire self that is cohesively decided. You get to live as independently and conjunctively as you choose. Just think of the healings you will experience encapsulated in one whole state of growth. This growth has huge, positive, multiplying effects. We cohesively, in body and soul, agree to marry our soul and ego as commitment to grow together. In this union, we come to know on a deep level that neither world poses a threat to our unique existence or a loss in exposing our authentic identity or, even more mind blowing, who we are yet to become!

What a thought! What a breakthrough! If we are steadfast and remain strong, consistent, and fearless, we have all the security we need to take this leap of faith and walk hand in hand with The Divine and stay rooted on this earth. We can use all our collective gifts, graces, and combined education from Divine Source. With this awareness, our soul joins us in a celebration, living a healthy union of combined energy. We do not have to be separated; we can choose to move with the mass; we can choose to be the mass; and we can choose to take a time out for reflection.

This wishing is mostly from what our ego thinks we deserve, need, or want. We have full reign to ask for the power to attract to us the wishes we desire. However, it is been my experience that not all my wishes have been granted. I have come to understand the universe wants me to have all the desires of my heart and soul.

However, there may be a wiser advisement going on pertaining to my intentions and in my best interests. This loving existence knows all and sees past, present, and future.

Universal love has a different out-of-body existence. It is a collective, conjunctive energy that spans time and dimension. In human containers, we could not possibly understand until we return home in spirit state. So, if I am not granted one of my wishes and wonder why the wish has not manifested, I am learning to accept that there is something far greater taking place, resulting always in my best interests or the best interests of the person for whom I was wishing. It never stops me from asking for the desires of my heart or for a request for another heart. I have just come to be patient with the granting of gifts, with a wise heart, full of knowledge, accepting the outcome.

How can this whole concept of sharing not be inspirational and life changing? If you choose to share from your cup, filling another cup, you continue to flow and grow, gaining the momentum of healing in your own experience. Learning the context of your life, gathering connections available, all you have do you is commit to it, say yes, and remain open to receive. I tell you again: if you could choose from my cup and pick anything you wish, I would give it freely with an open heart and soul. I know this truth as I experience life bearing witness time and time again to endless miracles, recycling back, flowing from Divine Spirit to divine person, reappearing in new form, validating, confirming a deeper commitment of life.

You normally do not receive the same things you give away to put back in your cup. Typically, you receive new gifts to offer the person asking. I did mention this before, but felt it important to repeat that this is part of the larger lesson when you have your own healing. This creates a wave of love so immense that it can cause reactions all around the world. Many battles that we are not even aware of are fought and won on our behalf spiritually. We have no need to understand this momentum of energy that keeps the healing in movement. We just need to trust the intentions with all we are: the purity of true love intended in our best interests, always. Free fall into this energy and wrap yourself around the effects and healing it creates for your personal experience.

Pay attention to your feelings. Be prepared if you say yes, you will be invited to join this universal life force of action that your team needs from you. You will feel the fountain bubble up within, recognizing your eternal life. Your spiritual team relies on you to get the messages being sent to encourage and inspire new growth. You will then witness what is happening in your own cup. Do not let this worry you, as teams of angels are designated to you personally to work with you on your journey. The universal life force is equipped to handle every single situation we are going to run into. You and your fellow beings are wonderful messengers; the team designated from The Divine, your ambassadors, their very existence personally chosen to help you. The only thing left for you to do is to simply ask, then accept their gifts with a gracious heart.

I would ask you to prepare yourself by simply being completely honest, with defined descriptions of the desires of your heart. What is the absolute best interest of your soul? What is your mission? What are your lessons? What will make you happy? What will complete you? What will deplete you? Know what it is you need and be very descriptive and explicit. Write out your desires to confirm on paper what you know to be honest and true. How can a universe that wants to give you everything and anything you desire really and truly know what to give you unless you know?

You have the power to manifest your dreams into your own realities by envisioning them. Continue to commit daily by asking for these gifts, asking for your guides and angels to come to you in dream state, helping you to attain your complete wholeness. This is a process and takes time to cultivate, understand, digest, and manifest. As you start to receive answers you have been looking for, you will discover their own special recipe, providing ingredients to help you grow into the envisioned whole of you. You start to take things less personally, claiming you, "your worth" and what belongs to you.

I would give anyone anything they asked for if it was of pure and honest heart. I have learned through this self-discovery that I no longer offer advice. I wait and I listen and I "give all" if called upon. I am a channel for divine truth for anyone seeking, anyone asking. Then we both, as a team of wise spirit and flesh, act as a direct channel of hope and trust, aiding in the awakening of the healer within you.

We are love. We are miracles of life, and we are here to connect and grow into magnificence, attained through the simplest form: a human being that is connected to a soul, entwined as one living being. We are a never-ending creation of continuous life. There is no room for fear; it just clouds our vision. We get to have as many chances as we wish to experience anything we need. Live, love, laugh - larger than you ever dared to! Life is coming at you. Choose to embrace it, or not; always your choice. If you do choose to embrace this life, love like you're on fire. It takes a brave person to test the waters, embrace the force, instead of resisting the power. Allow your body to filter this wisdom and fill your cup. Continue to be the messenger of loving source. You are perfect; you come from love; you will return to love. All things are forgiven, all things forgotten; learning your lessons and letting them go. There is so much more to experience, and you will recycle and return, learning new information pertinent to your existence. Be blessed, know blessed, and live blessed! We will, in all ways, stay connected in our hearts. Know this to be true: Divine love never leaves us stranded!

Cup Full Of Crystals

If you ever have the slightest curiosity to venture into a quiet little town nestled in between London and Sarnia, Ontario, you might discover Strathroy's charm and surprising appeal. We have two grocery stores, as well as several little, quaint, home-spun shops. One of these shops keeps calling my heart to check in. It is called Gypsy Soul Trading Co.

This unique shop has its own living heartbeat, which carries on in the tradition and lineage of family history. The proprietor, Tanya Griffin's heritage, her birthright, confirms this, as her shop is right beside what, for many years, was her grandfather's shop. I often wonder just how much time Tanya hung out there growing up as child. Her grandfather, Nick Homerodian, was our town's local shoe repairman and ran a successful business. Nick's Shoe Repair Shop was no ordinary shop, and Nick was no ordinary man. Nick could fix anything: belts, purses, coats - this man could do it all, often bringing old, broken items with emotional attachments back to a new life with new purpose. Nick had a love and passion for God that he wore like a steadfast breastplate of unconditional love. His brilliant smile and gentle, kind demeanor never wavered or changed. No matter how busy he was, he always took the time to make a person feel cared for.

Tanya, like her grandfather, is driven. She is making her mark and works harder than anyone I know. On summer weekends when Strathroy's main streets host a local farmers' market, Tanya is up in the very early hours of the morning while the town is still drenched in sleep. She prepares for the crowd by baking scores of pies, cookies, tarts, breakfast sandwiches, and designer cakes. She is an artist by trade; a master of her craft. Some of her spectacular cakes could showcase on Cake Boss. Yes, she is that good! I have come to discover that passion and hard work go hand in hand to create success. In Tanya's case, her lineage and love of her roots have built her business, much like the way her grandfather did.

A bit more about Tanya: she is lucky; she stands five feet tall, but there is absolutely nothing small about this wild gypsy, white witch soul! She moves to her unique heartbeat, drum, and drive, calling her artistically to anyone who needs her help. Tanya functions with a sound mind and the heart and soul of a sage to assist artists, creators, and energy workers for the better health and awakening of mankind through tools and magic. Tanya embraces magic and rituals of educational enlightenment passed down through the centuries. She delves deeply into something that calls her soul to healing and new life. She is always creating and rearranging her own shop to take on consignment proprietors, and also has a keen mind to expand, enhance, and create new income for her own in-house business. Every week, Tanya selects a well-thought-out menu, then posts it for something she calls The Sunday Dinner Club. This dinner club has become quite a growing business as well, independent from Gypsy Soul.

Tanya's creative retail space, Gypsy Soul, can be found at 78 Frank Street. Up until the fall of 2018, you would have been welcomed by her great big heart and a dog she lovingly addressed as "Goo" who was as big as she is. Goo was a gentle giant and a fixture we all came to cherish. Her store showcases delectable sweets in a big glass freezer and shelves of beautiful, hand-spun treasures of all sorts. And my first book, <u>Innerspace,</u> proudly has a spot that she rotates to different locations in the shop. She also has shelves of crystals of all shapes and sizes, and she falls in love with all of them. Tanya holds a passion for crystals and all the healing they provide, and she willingly shares that information with anyone who asks for her assistance. She often goes through the vendors who have shelf space in Gypsy Soul and buys "new babies," as she lovingly refers to them, before they even find their way for sale. She has her own personal collection and, on full moons, gathers up all her children so they can be washed in the love of a full moon; bathed, cleansed, and purified all over again.

I can still recall the day I met this Gypsy Soul. It was an instant love connection, and it was apparent in many ways she had an open heart, mind, and hunger to create and share her beautiful space with like-minded, passionate people.

As you have come to know me through my writing and methods of healing, there are many different ways to fill our cups. It is so great to share with others and let others share with us, and so, I have asked Tanya to share her journey with crystals. As you follow along, you will find out why she loves what she does and the reasons she is so devoted to crystal healing.

My personal knowledge of what crystals can and might do for you is limited. I know what feels good for me as I pick and choose the crystals I feel called to wear. For me, it always goes this way: My love for crystals is pure and instant. I usually wear a bracelet, and sometimes two at a time. Inevitably for me, I feel called to share them. I purchase the crystal, I take it off, and pay it forward as it has served a time of space and healing for me and must move on to aid another soul. And yes, I always know, and yes, it is always perfectly received for another heart to fill with white light and crystal love.

Please enjoy and receive Tanya and her testimonial of self-discovery on her journey with crystals and the hidden powers they possess.

In Tanya's words:

A little bit about me. I was brought up in the same little town where I still live. Raised as a Christian Baptist, I learned to crave ritual. By the time I reached my early teens, I found myself being pulled in a new and exciting direction. I had always had an interest in the mystics; after all, my name, Gryphon (variant of Griffin), means "queen of the fairies." Trolls and goblins and the Fae inspired me. I began to study the history of the first religion, paganism, and knew right away that this was the path for me. I believe it is a true connection to the Goddess, being at one with the earth and all its magic. I like to use food, crystals, and spells in the sharing of good energy, a natural form of therapeutic insight for any heart open to accepting these gifts. I am an artist every way you look at it. I work hard every day to help fill cups with beautiful things to look at that might bring you joy, cakes to help celebrate any occasion, food that fills your soul. I am a skill collector (I trade and exchange), a maker, a healer. I am a work in progress!

I believe in good energy and I love helping others in good energy to discover their paths. I bear witness to the most magical things on my own journey and commit to working alongside The Divine to teach, inspire, and co-operate with our Mother Earth's wisdom keepers. This is my path and my mantra:

Positive Minds, Positive Vibes, Positive Life

I would like to share a few things with you about how I discovered parts of myself on this crazy, crystal-filled adventure. This all started for me at the age of eleven after my parents decided to divorce, which landed me at weekly family therapy sessions. I am sure, looking back, I was more than a tad bitter, even a little hurt, and this made for a very awkward first session. In fact, I was a total jerk: arms crossed, full-on pout, bitch face! I had the hardest time opening myself up to our counsellor, even during one-on-one sessions. I mean, after all, it was not my divorce!

This is where it all changed for me. The session was ending, time to go. The counsellor led me towards his giant desk, which was full of interesting puzzles and gadgets, to a large, round basket full of tiny, tumbled stones. I choose one that appealed to me: Blue Tiger's Eye, he explained, and went on to tell me this stone was exactly what I needed to help me open up at our next session. The stone was going to provide me with mental clarity and focus, and help me find a way to resolve problems objectively. He then went on to say that this stone dispelled fear, as well as anxiety, and that it was a power stone. He said in the next session I would have all the power. Nuts, right? Crazy! As if a tiny rock was going to give me any power at all! Oh, I heard his words - I just did not believe him.

A full week went by, and I kept my new stone with me all the time. I loved playing with it. There was just something about feeling its smoothness between my fingers. I can't explain it, but it was calming. Could it really be working? I felt like a different person. I was somehow stronger. I seemed to own my voice. I felt confident and safe. It couldn't be that crystal!

Our next counselling session was amazing! I was able to work through my issues and open myself up. It was eye opening! I received a new crystal at the end of every session, and I was hooked!

My adventure working with crystals has been both empowering and stimulating. Back when I was first learning about crystals, there was no "Google" and it was a challenge finding any information or written books on this subject. I kept this path mostly to myself, taking long hikes to the library after I purchased a new crystal to do the research on it. It was during these solitary moments of connections that crystals and I developed a long and lasting relationship, getting to know one and other. I felt a comfort and bonding in this new-found, earthly power.

How would one start their own crystal journey? Filling your cup using the power of crystal energy all starts with a connection. This connection begins and ends with Mother Nature. These powerful tools have grown within her womb to serve us. She will help unite this divine connection between you. If you choose to respect this relationship and the gift, you will then discover and feel the power of this connection through you. Watch and feel your cup overflow with gifts of wisdom and aged love with the help of the Goddess, Mother Nature and her ancient, wise, absolutely gorgeous messengers!

Here is how a person might begin to tap into this mystic tool, which has surrounded us since the beginning of time. First, we need to understand what a crystal is. Crystals account for eighty percent of the earth's crust. They are made up of two elements: silicon and oxygen. Silicon conducts energy - we use it in technology every day. Quartz is found in computers, watches, phones; you name it, there is probably crystal technology involved.

I learned about crystals when I was young – believing is easier when you are younger, with an open mind and not all grown up yet. I find teaching children about crystal healing is so much easier because they are more open to magic. Need more convincing? Unfortunately, you do not get to physically see the crystal working for you. Results aren't immediate, and because they choose their timing of awakening, that can tend to turn off adults. Intentions need to be set, steps of respect need to be initiated; then its time to manifest.

I would like to share with you an example of a crystal power experience of a young boy. I met him at our downtown trick-or-treat event. The shop was full of all sorts of ghosts, princesses, and zombies. It was packed! I chose to gift crystals as well as candy and tried to explain a bit about the crystal each child chose. After the event was over, a mother and her six-year-old warrior ninja son returned to the shop to receive more information about the crystal he picked. I told her about how the Amethyst would calm his mind and the Obsidian would help block any negative energy surrounding him. She thanked me for my time and the information and went on her way.

That night, I received a text message exclaiming that for the first time in what seemed like forever, her son had gone to bed on his own and had been well behaved and helpful for the entire evening before going to bed. A miracle in her eyes! Her son had some severe attention deficit issues, and she was taken aback by the results of these crystals. Now, we do a weekly healing session at the shop to help manage his impulses, as well as work with crystals to still his overactive mind.

Picking Your Cyrstal

Start quietly; shut out the world for just one minute; take a small time out and focus. What is the problem? How are you feeling? Begin to trust these feelings manifesting, coming to an awareness as you focus on the crystals placed around you. This awareness might start with the colour of a crystal, perhaps the shape; you will be drawn to some and turned off by others. Let your intuition be your guide and allow yourself to feel their energy. Pick up one at a time and hold your crystal in your hand. Feel the weight of it, the texture, the size.

Take a few moments to reflect. How does it feel to reflect? Move on to the next crystal you were drawn to and so on, and try to be mindful that you do not overwhelm yourself with choice. I like to choose three options; trinity, meaning three spiritually speaking, has always been a power number for me. Let your intuition whisper to you, then choose. Trust yourself that you chose the crystal you were drawn to for the lesson and healing you need. Deep down, within, we all know what our soul is asking for. At times, it is just so hard to access that information without awareness and focus on our healing and growing needs.

Sometimes, it takes a while for your crystals to get to know you. Some people experience full body vibrations; some people feel a change in temperature, immediate joy, or the emotion of sadness; sometimes you feel nothing at all. Everyone's connection to crystal energy will be a unique and personal experience.

A friend of mine can "be at one" with a crystal from the first moment of touch. It is so emotional for me to watch how he becomes one with the crystal, combining his own physical energy. Another friend felt nothing from most crystals; then one day was knocked on her ass by a piece of Calcite. This piece of Calcite now has a place of honour and sits on the pillow beside her every night.

You may want to consider being of open mind to crystal energy, respecting this bewitching gift from the The Divine herself. Consider slowing down your thoughts in meditation with a few crystals by your side. Connect to this energy, allowing the wisdom to fill your cup with the help of Mother Nature. I practice this every morning, with every confidence that I am whole and at one with The Divine and we, together, are choosing the right crystals for whatever challenges lie ahead in my day.

Crystal Care / Assign A Mission

Once you have chosen your new crystal, you need to give it a purpose. Here is where we learn to set an intention and assign your crystal its mission, sometimes called programming. This action is needed to establish a solid intention.

Cleansing your crystal requires you to first cleanse the space you occupy with your crystals and yourself of any negative or stale energy. I prefer to use sage or Palo Santo wood to cleanse the area with a smudging session. Cleansing your space can be a useful tool if you have had a gathering of people in your home or personal space, after harsh words have been exchanged, or you have had a run of bad luck, especially if you have been ill. Cleanse the crystal the same way; slowly pass the crystal through the smoke of your smudge source three times. Smudging in this way is super effective for anytime usage of your crystal. I personally prefer the power of the full moon to cleanse my crystals. Mother Earth and Sister Moon are constantly looking out for us and spread a celestial wash of energy over our crystal life tools. Some crystals work like sponges; other types work like batteries. Every once in a while, they need a good wringing out or a recharge in order to work effectively.

Setting An Intention

Setting an intention is an important step in crystal working. Start by asking yourself what you need to fill your cup full of goodness. What is missing? What do you desire? Even more personal, what do you deserve? What are your values, goals, aspirations? What commitment is it going to take for you to achieve fulfillment?

Once you have spent some time reflecting on these desires, put your crystals to work. Be as specific as you can be, considering everything it would take for all this to swing in your favour and highest good. Write it down and then meditate on this and whatever specifics you are asking for, believing entirely that you deserve it. Command your crystals to go to work on your specific intentions. Again, I like to break my intentions up into three, using the power of the trinity to assist in holding the crystal's newly-designated, specific vibration. Repeat this ritual three times. It is imperative not to forget to thank The Divine three times, as well. What you are asking for already exists within the universe. Send out your own vibrational echo to Mother Earth to honour your newly-set intention. Now, take some time out to reflect. Be filled with gratitude. Be patient and watch in wonder as your internal cup begins to flow with some seriously good healing energy.

The moon plays a huge roll in timing with crystals, and you may want to plan to set some intentions on the new moon. It is the perfect time to get the ball rolling, working with moon magick and your crystals in a combination of powerful, combined energy to amplify your healing.

Dealing With Negative Energy

Every single one of us has an aura. How I would describe an aura is that it is a bubble of energy, helping to keep you in balance. Our aura is being constantly challenged! People, computers, televisions, cell phones, all are different forms of energy connections that try to steal or drain your internal cup. When you feel off, weak, drained, or frustrated, it may be more than likely your energy was being invaded. I know this to be my truth because I am empathic, which allows me to be aware of the repairing of my own aura. I use crystals to rebuild and repair my own bubble of protection. I use Kyanite or Tourmaline or Obsidian, as these powerhouse crystals will cut through any form of negative energy. Clear Quartz will help establish healing to your aura. Pyrite is also a powerful aura shield.

Negative energy does not stop at sabotaging your emotional wellbeing; it can enter our living spaces, as well. In my busy little store downtown, full of crystals, sage, and magick this and thats, I like to smudge at the end of every day to clear out any residual negativity. The next time you feel off, trust in the embrace of divine love and that she has your back. We all have a darkness we have taught ourselves to repress. These heavy emotions serve no purpose and eventually need to be released. You can assist with the release of these toxins by using Ruby Zoisite or Shungite. Open your heart to the darkness; accept it; then smudge yourself. Stay connected to the earth energy, and divine energy will continue to consistently work with you to aid the growth of your personal development. You cannot control negativity; however, this will help you keep this energy in check and also help you prepare for whatever chaos the day may throw at you.

A full cup! Every day!

Now that you have a better understanding about the energy and power your crystals harness, it is time to learn to use them! Crystals are gorgeous, and it may be that simply admiring them is use enough for you at first, but after you get to know them a little, start assigning them a purpose. Here are a few of the ways I assign crystals every single day.

Infusion

To describe to you how infusion of crystals might work, I refer to infusing like tea. I use it in all sorts of applications. Take your daily water intake, for instance. Crystals' vibrational frequencies have the ability to change the structure and quality of the molecules in the water, so why not improve your water with a little crystal energy? Add Rose Quartz for a love vibration, Citrine for an uplifting vibe, Smoky Quartz for some grounding, Amethyst for aches and pains or headaches; Shungite has been known to have the ability to purify water of almost all organic matter, like metals, bacteria, and even pesticides and harmful micro-organisms.

I don't just infuse my drinks. To further the respect I have and the power they wield, I infuse my bath water and my food, as well. Nothing beats a nice, relaxing, hot soak in a tub full of lavender and Himalayan salt to put yourself at ease. You might try adding some Amethyst or Amazonite and become one with the water vibes. On a dull, grey, cold, wintry day, my favourite "pick me up" is some citrus oils and a handful of Citrine crystals. Nothing going your way? Luck not on your side? Pyrite and Jade's combination can be known to enhance prosperity. Heck - go ahead and add the Citrine to that too!! There are times when I find myself in a rut of negativity - either the energy around me or my very own vibe just will not give me a break! In those times, I tend to jump into a tub full of Smoky Quartz and Obsidian. This action tends to wash all the negativity away. After my soak, I use some Palo Santo wood or some sage or a lavender wand to clear the energy in my bathroom.

When it comes to the creation of preparing food, I take infusion very seriously. I am a true gypsy-kitchen witch, not shy about setting intentions and casting spells or making elixirs out of my soups and sauces. I have created a weekly dinner club, where every week I feed dozens and dozens of families. These menus are created with awesome, home-cooked meals, loaded with amazing intentions for the week. Prosperity, love, good fortune, good health: all these pre-intentions can be achieved by showing your food a little crystal love beforehand. I use a ton of Clear Quartz in my cooking. I believe its the strongest stone out there, said to work on any condition, connecting you to your higher self. It can amplify any intention or energy.

Crystal Gridding/ Intention Setting

In my previous paragraphs I touched a bit on intention setting, giving a specific crystal a specific job, but what if there was a way to amplify it all - manifest your biggest goals, your deepest desires? The relationship of crystals to other crystals forms a union of energy, especially when combined with a geometric pattern. Be a witness to your manifestation resulting from a quicker, powerful, combination. I would like to share something personal as an example.

I filled out an application for the rescue of a gorgeous four-year-old Saint Bernard, which was a crazy, hard decision because of the recent loss of my squishy-faced, familiar Brutus. Something kept telling me to go for it. Everything about this felt right! Although it was a crazy, long, stressful, three-week process, I continued with full intentions on this being MY dog. I set a small crystal grid under my till at the shop. Along with the manifestation, I decided to squirrel away every fifty and one-hundred-dollar bill I made until I saved up the five-hundred-dollar fee for the adoption. I tried to stay positive, even though the rescue had been shared on social media over 300 times. Although hundreds of other families wanted to adopt him, I felt positive about the outcome. I believe in my heart I was the one who had put in the energy work. In fact, I believed I fully deserved him and he deserved me. Long story short, the day I managed to save my last fifty dollars was the day the agency called to say that he was ours!!! *Insert goose bumps here, ha ha!!*

Pendulums/Answer Tellers

A pendulum is a useful tool when you need help delving a little deeper into your self-conscience. Once you have a trained pendulum, confirming decisions becomes so much easier. You can use it to help you make a purchase, verify a decision, answer yes and no questions and more. Pendulums are often used in healing. The energy found in a swinging pendulum is like a concentrated beam of vibrations that can help with pain or inflammation by directly holding it above the problem area and letting it focus its strength there.

Crystal Touch

Okay! This is exciting for me, as this is my favorite way to use crystals! Literally touch - crystal massage! I love collecting crystals that you just know are going to feel great on your skin. I have palm shaped, wand shaped, spheres, and rollers. We already know about crystals' frequencies and vibrations, so why not put them to use for us when we need a little touch healing? I have a Selenite wand that feels just amazing when rubbed directly on either side of my spine. I have an Obsidian and a Jade roller I like to use on my face before bed. Asian cultures have been using Jade rollers for centuries. Tension causes wrinkles and fine lines that this tool can prevent, not to mention puffiness and under-eye circles.

My newest adventure in crystal healing? Yoni eggs! Yup. As in "up my yoni." A woman's magic all starts in her womb. It is her power. We, as women, have a responsibility to honour and respect her. She has been through it all: Intercourse, childbirth, menstruation. Life happens! She is yours to protect. I had an awakening a few months back, where I had substantially more than a dribble with no warning, no feeling; it just surprised me with a wet leg. I am only 36 years old, so you can imagine how frightened I was by this scenario. I started looking for answers right away and found the yoni egg. This egg has been used since ancient times for improving the spiritual and physical health of women. Use this crystal egg regularly to tone your pelvic floor muscles for better bladder control, enhance your vaginal health, and yes, an even stronger connection to self-love, manifesting increased, powerful orgasms.

I hope that some - or any - or all of this information hits home with you, in the middle of your heart. Crystals work tirelessly to rid your body, mind, and soul of blockages. I have set an intention to your entire being to have the courage to expand and be open to drinking in the silent power of Mother Earth's stunning healers. Find reasons to let them be a part of your life and witness the magic begin, healing you, filling your cup to an abundance of overflowing health and wholeness.

Cup Full Of Wand

I first met Natasha Ohler while still working at my last full-time job, when she decided to come in to the office to discuss a warranty issue. I was able to listen and advise her on our policy and procedure. She was concerned about the timeline and felt comfortable enough to tell me that she had suffered a bad concussion, which had held her up for a few months on dealing with this issue.

Since our initial meeting, I am happy to say Natasha Ohler is a very big part of my journey and soul work, and connected, we share. I remember our initial meeting. She came in and we talked for a very long time. The content of this conversation was an instant reminder of why I love energy and why I love working with it so very much. She brought me the best present - a heart-shaped rock she had picked up in her travels. I think she found it at the beach she loves at Kincardine, Ontario. I remember her being very shy and nervous when she handed me this precious stone, and as many who have come to know me have also come to know, I keep very little without giving it away or passing on the energy it can provide for someone else to help them mend or heal. For some reason, I have never been able to part with this rock and it follows me from place to place. Now, that does not mean I will not pick it up one day and give it to a new home; however, I make few promises about that kind of commitment. When I give, it is more of a calling and a direct command - usually a bit of a battle - but in the end it is paying it forward.

Natasha is a one of the most authentic, gifted teacher/healers I have ever been privileged to work with, and together we support conjunctive healing and combined gifts. She is educated, refined, and authentic. She is an animal communicator, a human facilitator, and she has a vast knowledge and many varied designations of accreditation. She holds a Master's Degree in Reiki and is a Karuna practitioner. She has studied Access Consciousness, Jikiden Reiki certification, Therapeutic Touch, and Crystal Awakening Certification. She has completed many other courses of interest, all pertaining to natural, gentle alternatives to promote healing.

It is pretty safe to say that, over time, Natasha and I have developed very close soul and personal relationships. She and I would exchange energy work over the phone and in person. We have had many, many stories and miracle moments of healing, with the connection of The Divine, who provided loving, angelic forces in the delivering of divine messages to and for each other. Natasha - yes, she will tell you I almost always call her 'Tash' - shares these gifts, thus supporting her vast amount of truth and accurate knowledge. She adores animals of all kinds and, more often than not, she feels animals love her without judgment. She communicates on their level and understands them as they communicate with her about many things.

I mentioned to Natasha that I had a dream, and it was a dream that was very real. The dream was about a healing circle, and there were people in this circle who were having experiences that were healing to them. In this dream, I was facilitating the healing and holding a healing wand. The wand, as I tried to describe to Tash, was beautiful and powerful and was the primary tool in this session that gave power to the person holding it to speak, ask, or just receive the loving energy that radiated from it. I felt very strongly that I was to share my dream and vision and asked Tash to create this healing wand I was to use to lead and facilitate the circle. I knew this wand was the key to helping many unlock what was inside and give them courage, or give them the tools to access their needs and desires through the circle and the ritual we were to create. I knew this transitioning movement was life altering, but had no idea how huge at the time.

So; as it goes, I did share this idea in a passionate phone conversation and then face to face. I know she was a bit overwhelmed with the whole idea, as well as the responsibility, but I also knew it was the key we needed and the elements required for the bonding and healing the circle would create for all.

Natasha sat with this concept for a while, and then it happened. She created a beautiful, sacred, powerful healing tool. I can remember the day she delivered the wand and handed it over. She came to my office and I was able to take some time away from my desk. She came with two other women who brought the gifts of joy and self as we prayed and shared the moment together. Then, the wand was given and received in the presence of a spirit-filled room. As I unwrapped the blanket like it was a living child, clear bubble wrap appeared, and as the layers revealed the wand in all its elements, power, and glory, I witnessed its birth, naked and raw, created for healing and healers of all walks and forms to discover the wealth of love and hope entwined in the wood, feathers, crystals, and copper. It vibrated in my hands, welcoming me and asking me to share the magnificence of the universe for all brave enough to want to hold it. The moment was frozen in time. In slow motion, we passed the gift of energy and healing life around the room.

This tool, this wand, was initiated in October 2017 at our very first healing circle at a store called Windell's Chocolate. The proprietor's name is May, and she believed in the whole process of what I do and what I work for. She has been a constant, loving, giving being. May offered her space, time, and love up to the healing circles we held at her shop. She was always making space for my book and my music, hosting two book signings at her location to allow me an opportunity to promote the passion I have for my work for divine love and purpose. She created beautiful events, serving hand-painted cookies with words from the book in a purple colour theme. May is incredible and talented and big hearted. Although the healing circle has changed locations as May has moved on to further her ambitions in life, the fact remains that May welcomed us with open arms, warm hot chocolate, coffee, and the best homemade Belgian chocolates the world has yet to discover. Her heart, soul, trust, and open arms made a difference in healing hearts in our healing circles.

The very first night, I had decided I would facilitate and lead the circle for three months; then, I would kindly offer the wand up and someone else could expand the pay-it-forward movement on the baton like a relay. I was quite proud of myself for setting that boundary. Those three months seemed to fly by. Many came, received, and found the courage to share while holding the wand that was passed from person to person in the circle of healing, protection, and love. Everyone in the circle who received from this powerful source of love could, and would, share their own personal story if they chose. Some did share how the power of the wand either gave them courage or touched them personally and deeply, knowing that The Divine and self were committed to the connection. I cannot speak for all, but I do feel them all with me, supporting this journey - our combined journey - all capable of working in conjunction through this connection of unity, labor, love, power, trust, and connection.

As the third month was coming to the end, the group asked if we could extend the intended three months a while longer. They did not want this group to end. It was quickly voted to keep going. At the time of writing, we were going into our eleventh month since inception. Sometime in May, our May came to us and said she had to close her doors. We were all sad for her, for the circle, for the community she had built, and the beautiful shop. She had built her business through hard work, blood, sweat, and tears, but in the end, she decided to close her doors and pursue something else. She was sad, we were sad, and we put it out at our last circle to all to see if they could find another location for us that was feasible to share gifts of our healing circle. The response was wonderful. We ended up with three options and all were willing to donate the space and their time. How wonderful! Not one, but three to choose from. For me, the trinity number three has always been my personal spiritual validation. We accepted a place called the Yoga Spot, a pleasant location with tons of windows and tons of healthy, holistic energy. We are grateful that we get to carry on and have space and a place to heal ourselves, expand, invite, and extend the energy as a collective gathering of good white love and light.

At every healing circle, we make time to pass the wand around the room for personal sharing of thoughts, reflection, or healing. Natasha often brings her wands, and people often feel called to purchase their own healing wand for gifts or for themselves. Truly, the wands call you. Ask anyone who reaches out to hold one.

Natasha will share her own words, in her own way, about the construction and tools she used to create and answer to the calling the wand had for her. I welcome you to open your whole being to her, as I did and will continue to do. I call her often in my spirit for healing and, most times, she knows I am calling her, often reaching out at the very same time, lovingly and consistently helping each other get to the next stage of our journey. She has enlightened and helped me on countless occasions, and I truly love her for all her gifts and the beauty she holds in her own cup for anyone who needs love and guidance.

In Natasha's words:

I have known Tracey for several years now. We met in a very unique way and there was a series of events that fell into order for us to talk the day we first spoke to each other over the phone, and then meet in person. We initially had a very nice talk over the phone and I had disclosed that I had been healing from a concussion. We found out that we both did Reiki, and we ended up doing a distance healing for each other that day. We had an instant connection. I knew when I finally went in to pick up my order a few weeks later that she was a soul connection for me. I am a very shy person and Tracey is not! We are total opposites! Tracey is an air sign, and I am very earthy. She kicks me when I need a push and makes me laugh when I am not expecting it and need it, and I think, perhaps, I teach her patience among other things. We have done some excellent healing work and growing together.

One day, she told me about her vision of a healing circle she wanted to start. She discussed her thoughts about the outline of how the circle would run, and she asked me (or told me!) that she wanted me to make a "healing tool." She wanted me to create a special tool with crystals that would be passed around the circle for each person to receive healing. Individuals would have the floor while holding the wand, to speak (or not) of anything they needed or wanted; perhaps to share, cry, ask for or maybe receive healing.

I was initially scared. I had no idea what to do, but I said, "Okay. Thank you for thinking of me and trusting me with this task!" I had no idea where to start, so I sat on it for a while. Backtracking many months, I had spent six afternoons over the winter, for several hours each day over several months, taking a crystal certification course at a store in downtown Toronto. We learned the science behind crystals, the healing properties, the different kinds of Clear Quartz crystals and their individual properties, how crystals affect and compliment our chakras, crystal grids, meditation, and the astrological connection to and with our signs and birth charts. We also learned how to harness energy associated with the different elements in crystals in relation to the sun and moon influence. I loved the time spent doing the hours of homework each night and each week: the research, the meditations, the journaling, and setting up grids. This all complimented and enhanced the energy work I had already been doing with my Reiki practice and the different modalities I was already practicing.

When Tracey asked me about a healing tool, I put into place all things, elements I wanted to see covered for the people experiencing different life issues. I started choosing crystals that covered the chakras and the elements that I had studied. The elements are also represented by a visible item, if possible, such as a feather for air/wind. Sometimes I find my own unique feathers, but I started sourcing organically-raised and gathered feathers from North America. It was also important to have an earth representation which also took different shapes, such as a butterfly or heart. I find these stones myself on the shores of Lake Huron, and occasionally on Lake Erie or Lake Ontario. My husband and children also know what I am looking for and help with the searches. We always bring home too much driftwood, too many rocks, beach glass, fossils, and wish stones (stones from the beach that have perfect circular lines around them).

For Tracey's healing tool, I also wanted extra grounding crystals and higher power and angelic connection crystals, amplifier quartz crystals, and stones for the heart, transformation, voice (throat chakra), courage, balance, etc. I knew I wanted to wrap it with copper wire because copper is an energy conductor. This way, all the stones, crystals, and pieces are appointed in such a way that it would not matter where you placed your hands. In fact, you would benefit from the entire wand and be connected to the conduit of collective energy while receiving what you need at that time, in that moment. I found the wire that I thought would work, and the next issue to solve was what was going to hold it all together. I looked through all the pieces of driftwood that we had and found a few that I thought might work. I finally settled on a piece of driftwood that I took from my son's room. He and I had found it together on the beach near Kincardine.

I placed the stones, crystals and chosen pieces on the driftwood and had to play with the placement of each one. Once I was happy with the order and overall look, I secured each piece and started to wrap it with the copper wire. It took me hours to wrap it, as I wanted it to be tightly wound and wrapped and perfect. I sat with it for several hours before I sent photos to Tracey. I knew that, like me, Tracey would need to see it in person and feel it, as well.

I am very grateful to Tracey for giving me an opportunity that has changed my life and allowed me to develop and explore my creative side. I have known for a long time that I needed to pursue the healer side of me, and I eventually left my employment of 26 years to do this. My children were getting older and it was the right time. I enjoy seeing the combinations of colours and stone and crystals and how they all work together. I love seeing it all come together, and I am still learning about what size, shape, and feel works with the different pieces of driftwood. I love doing Reiki, Access Consciousness, and the other work I do. The healing tool work has added an amazing element to my life that I never would have expected. Thank you, Tracey!

Cup Full Of Oil

I met Cate O'Neil on a day my spirit was directing me to use oil for healing. Yes, oil for healing is what my body was craving. Interesting, because I initially went into Cate's office to investigate her advertisement for laser weight loss. It was somewhat intriguing to me how the concept of a laser could aid a person in weight loss. So, I called Cate and asked if I could come to see her. She remembers the date we met - May 18, 2017. This was the day essential oils changed my life, my perspective, and my awareness on the healing properties they contain. That day, I met another earth angel!

Always on a mission, often trying to cram more than one project into another, I was out doing errands for work, made the call to Cate, and stopped in to check it out. The spa immediately calmed my hectic state. I stepped into Cate's office, and the oil that was wafting out of her diffuser was even more settling and calming. I remember she was on a call, and the receptionist kindly asked me if I could wait for a minute to see Cate. I looked around the spa and was quite curious about all the pendants hanging, with different coloured felt to go inside. I could see that the felt was used as a material to soak up oil, but thought it was more for fragrance than for healing.

When Cate came out of her office to greet me, I noticed she was stunning. She had the most beautiful, angelic smile that radiated from her heart and her soul. She has bright blue eyes that speak experience and education. It was clear to me from the moment we met, she was going to be my oil angel. I was in a rush, trying to cram an hour information meeting into a 'just give me what my soul knows I need' meeting. She took me and my certifiable craziness all in stride, not missing a beat. I told her I was there because my soul called me to go there, that she would know what I needed for healing, and she would just do that for me. She said, "okay" and proceeded to do what she always does, believes in, and, deep down, truly knows.

Cate runs her own reputable business that allows her freedom to use the products in the best way for her company and her clients. I know because I trust her, that she knows what I need and, if she is not sure, she researches it. I have come to love essential oils and do have a few favourites, like lavender at night in my diffuser by my side of the bed, spewing heavenly sleeping aid in our bedroom. My personal healing oil and go-to is Frankincense; yes, one of the gifts, so the story goes, to Baby Jesus at his birth from three very wise men! It is expensive, and it is worth every single healing drop it has to offer.

Since meeting Cate and getting to know her and her love and passion for this way of living, using oils daily, I have further investigated, as well as experienced some other uses. Last year, I was invited to work at my first Healing Body and Spirit Expo, held the second weekend of March every year in Kalamazoo, Michigan. This invitation was such an honour for me. Beverly Stephen, the creator and facilitator for the cover of my first book, _Innerspace_, is the reason I believe the spirit led me to working with her. Beverly, working with the North American Healing Circuit in her own highly successful business - "world renowned physic artist medium" - found there was a true need to organize and facilitate an expo of divine light workers. This Expo was created by combining a level of healing, authentic, connecting energy, providing a channel of divine love and light offering a higher frequency of love for those seeking true healing. Beverly's high energy, family dynamics, and spirit-led experience working with a higher frequency attracts many exhibitors. I happen to know that her Healing Body and Spirit Expos have a waiting list of credible and authentic healers standing in line for an opportunity to be a part of this work.

Beverly was eager to bring me into her spiritual family and arranged a booth at the Expo in March 2018. She added me to the program with two prime, half-hour lecture spots. To say I was nervous was the biggest understatement of my healing work to date, but The Divine has been calling me out to love His people on a wider platform for some time. I could feel The Divine tugging and calling my heart to feed His people, love His people. "One on one is so important and quite safe, secure, and comfortable," He whispered, "but larger groups with a message of love for everyone have amplified power." Trusted faith is what I held on to that weekend. It was much bigger than I am, and The Divine was teaching me that.

A couple of days before I went on the venture, Cate – yes, angel Cate – said, "Tracey, I want to gift you with an oil massage. You can go with a renewed sense of clean wholeness." Well, how can you say no to that kind of gift? So, I arrived at her house; she welcomed me and proceeded to saturate me with so many warm relieving sensations. I felt myself opening to receive it all. Cate's expert touch and specific oils turned my aching, over-thinking, working body into a pliable heap of freedom on so many levels. I did not understand it, but welcomed it in my entirety. The foot massage was incredible! I think I left my body for a few moments. The action of love, combining the massaging of the oils deep into my body and the power of the oils to aid in healing, gave me energy to get through that weekend of intensity.

This oil massage experience with Cate leads me also to share my pendulum experience with her. She was able to communicate with my body and help me unblock my chakras. That was an incredible experience as she quickly identified the blocks, and we used the oils she felt called to provide. Each of the oils she chose was accurate, relieving me of stress, anxiety, accumulated intestinal blockage, and many other things my body tends to hold on to. This was so powerful, I felt strongly that others needed to experience this form of healing, and, in August of 2018, Cate did a teaching at the healing circle; Cate, using oils and adding her pendulum; and another angel, Alicia, facilitating by vocally collaborating with Cate, explaining in detail the meaning, properties, and origin of the chakras. It was a powerful evening of combined education and healing put into practice.

I would now like to invite you all to read Cate's version of her healing world and the way it has forever changed her life through the use of oils, teaching Cate her life's purpose as it continues to manifest for her.

In Cate's words:

When I first used an essential oil, it was out of desperation. My sleep was slowly being consumed by night terrors so vicious that I was convinced I needed to seek out professional advice to help me cope.

While on a weekend women's retreat, I warned my roommates of my nighttime experiences so they would not be alarmed if I started shouting out in my sleep. Our retreat host mentioned that she had an essential oil that may help me – Lavender; not just any garden variety lavender, but an essential oil sourced around the world from plants with pure, therapeutic value. Being a true skeptic about natural healing, my first response would normally be to dismiss her suggestion, but I was desperate! I bought the Lavender.

Two weeks later, I was a believer! After applying the Lavender to the bottoms of my feet every night for 2 weeks, the night terrors were gone! This just couldn't be a coincidence – could essential oils really help? That revelation started me on my journey to share essential oils.

As science is getting closer to discovering the pathways that allow essential oils to work within our bodies, for me, there is still somewhat of a mystery surrounding the oils. While one oil will be the perfect answer to help with a certain condition – as Lavender helped with my night terrors – it may not have the same effect on someone else. In fact, it may have exactly the opposite effect! Reference books are great guides in recommending choices of oils for different concerns and conditions, but I believe there is something more.

It is embarrassing to confess my first reaction to Reiki and the art of Healing Touch. About 25 years ago, I remember listening to a conversation where a career nurse was working in the Recovery Room and describing a woman who came to see a patient at the family's request. I joined in the laughter and disbelief at how waving one's arms over a body could, in any way, heal where all the advances of science and modern medicine could not. A few years later, I found out just how wrong I could be. At a convention in Toronto, I had a bad fall and severely sprained my ankle. A trip to the Emergency Room determined that my ankle wasn't broken, but it was so swollen and painful I had to use crutches. I was aware that one of my roommates for that weekend was a Reiki healer, but I had absolutely no idea what that was. The moment we got back to the room, she was performing healing touch on my ankle. As I felt what I can only describe as energy shifts within my body, I had flashbacks to the conversation about the Recovery Room patient. The next morning, I left the crutches in the room and walked on my own again. I realize this is less than remarkable in terms of healing, but for me I experienced my first 'ah ha' moment! There was so much more to healing than the modern medicine I had relied on all my life.

The next part of my journey of awakening is more difficult to describe. I had been using and sharing oils with all my family and friends, so much so that it was becoming part of my business and nicely complimented my stop smoking laser service. I feel a strong sympathy for people I meet, especially if they are hurting or ill, and I believe that essential oils may help them. I stay well stocked in sample bottles! These I offer to clients if they are open to trying essential oils. Then came the day I met Tracey, and my world started to open!

As I shared oils with her and our friendship developed, she invited me to join a healing circle she was facilitating. I said I would attend, but realized when I checked my calendar that I was double booked that evening with another event. I have come to learn that there is no such thing as coincidence! Ten minutes before that healing circle was to begin, my prior event cancelled due to illness and I was free to attend my first healing circle. There is no logic to explain what I experienced that evening. While holding Tracey's wand as it was passed around the circle, I felt an electricity shooting up my arms. The second time I held the wand, it practically jumped out of my outstretched hands. There was a message here and I started to listen.

Since my initial experience with Lavender, I have witnessed firsthand many occasions when essential oils have helped someone. I would like to share my 'Frankincense' story, as I now call it.

Twenty years ago, I suffered a spinal cord infarct called Transverse Myelitis. This incident left me paralyzed on my right side below my waist and with no feelings of touch, temperature, or pain in my left leg. I am forever grateful that I was able to regain the ability to walk again and have only a few lingering issues. Chronic pain, however, is one of those issues. This is kept under control mainly with medication, but every so often I experience debilitating 'break through' pain in my chest. Before essential oils, this would necessitate a trip to the Emergency Room for stronger pain medication. Then, I discovered the power of Frankincense. One night around 2:00 a.m., the pain hit. My husband was getting dressed to drive me to the hospital when I told him no, I was going to use my oils instead and reached for my Frankincense. I asked Paul to place drops of the oil all up my back along my spine, and then to gently massage it in. Following a friend's advice, I also massaged Lavender over my heart to relieve the stress and help me relax. Within 30 minutes the pain was easing, and after an hour it was gone. My faith in the power of essential oils strengthened.

While I share the oils, I also share my knowledge, helping people understand their many uses and how to apply them. My first introduction to chakras came at the women's retreat I attended. My friend Cathy, our weekend host, led a class on chakras, demonstrating how different crystals and colours can allow closed chakras to open and spin, thereby allowing your body's energy to flow more freely. I was totally intrigued! When Cathy was offering a class on chakras and essential oils, I was front row centre, soaking up all the knowledge I could. I started assisting Cathy with the classes, gradually gaining enough confidence in my abilities to lead classes on my own.

Eventually, the more people with whom I connected to test their chakras and suggest an essential oil that would unblock closed chakras, the more I became aware of a greater power guiding this process. Approximately 90 percent of the time, the first oils that I was suggesting proved to be the ones the clients needed. This was defying the laws of probability! Tracey invited me to speak at one of the healing circles to talk about chakras and oils. At the close of the presentation, I offered to test the chakras of anyone who wanted to try it. I tested 21 guests that evening and, in every instance, the first oil I suggested was the correct one for them. There can be no explanation other than Divine guidance. It was not my hand alone that was reaching for the bottle of oil.

One of the services I offer in my clinic is the AromaTouch® Technique developed by Dr. David K. Hill, D.C. This technique involves the application of specific essential oils combined with human touch to provide an uplifting essential oils experience, and allows me to connect with a client on an emotional level. I love offering the AromaTouch® Technique, as I receive almost as much benefit from the essential oils as does my client. Rarely does a client not experience positive energy during a session.

As my journey of awakening continues, I am so very grateful for the blessings I have received along the way. I have met so many new people who I am honoured to call friends; new friends who open doors to new ideas and/or experiences that enrich my soul. At a recent healing circle, I experienced my first drumming session, which was amazing and powerful beyond words. I've been introduced to Orgonites and their healing power, and oracle cards and their messages. Through this journey winds the power of essential oils.

While scientific research continues, I am intrigued by the Divine connection to essential oils. Even though I don't understand it or can't express what it is, I feel a connection with some people, even when meeting them for the first time. It is as if I know what oil to reach for to help them. This isn't a feeling I can turn on or off, and I don't know why it happens with certain people and not others, but I'm learning to simply accept that it happens and follow my instincts. I recall a conversation with a colleague when she described seeing a white aura around me. I remember feeling embarrassed and almost fraudulent. I have never even come close to seeing auras and couldn't understand how someone could see one around me. Tracey was a party to this conversation, however, and glanced over at me with such a sweet smile that I knew it was true.

Where this journey is leading me, I can't begin to know. Of one thing I am certain – I am open to following the path. That first bottle of Lavender has opened so many doors into the remarkable world of essential oils and beyond. I will be forever grateful to Cathy Brown-Swanton for making the introduction.

Essential Oils do not cure disease. They do not prevent illness. They only help your body heal itself.

Cup Full Of Orgonite

How Reiki led me to Orgonites – *by Maria Webb*

My healing journey started at the end of 2012, when I went into real estate to earn a living without taking a lot of time away from my two small children. At the time, I had three children from 1 year old to 20 years old. After being at home for three years with small children, I felt voiceless and powerless in my own home. I was sick and tired of being tired ALL the time. All I thought about was getting a nap after a long day of chasing two children under the age of 3.

Around that time, I watched the movie, "The Secret," which led to my reading The Success Principles by Jack Canfield. I also listened to the audiobook, Life Visioning by Michael Bernard Beckwith (MBB). I thought my issue was lack of planning, so I followed Jack Canfield. I felt that if I had a strict schedule and a plan, I would earn my own money and get my power and voice back without sacrificing time with my children.

I kept on this path, seeking training on processes and systems to improve my business practices. This led me to joining a local real estate firm that I believed had an excellent training system for realtors. Still thinking that efficiency and money would buy me more time to get fit and have more energy, I stayed on this path from January 2013 to August 2016, when I met Tracey, who was planning to list her condo in Michigan. As we were heading into the winter season, we discussed listing the property in the spring when more buyers start looking for vacation properties. We did not talk again until February 4, 2017. In the meantime, the children were now in school, and I started seeing a chiropractor for chronic back and shoulder pain. Up until this point, I had spent most of my time reading business coaching books. These books provided little information on mindset and a lot on process. I was getting sicker. I was going to the chiropractor on a monthly basis for adjustments and had started going to an acupuncturist.

This is where my journey picks up speed. Most of this journey happened through the magic of social media on Facebook. Through a Facebook event, I saw that Tracey was having a book signing in Lexington, so out of curiosity, I went. I had a wonderful talk with her and drew an angel card. She said, "This message is for you. Take a picture of it and meditate on it." The card read:

> <u>A blessed idea.</u> An idea manifests endless blessings but you must act to bring the idea to life. The time is right. Know that the world is full of ideas floating around aimlessly until someone notices and breathes life into them. This is your time to shine. Have faith.

I took a picture of the card and bought Tracey's first book and CD and took them home. Then, I really started thinking, "What is my blessed idea?"

The next Facebook event that caught my eye was a mastermind on John Maxwell's book, <u>Put Your Dream to the Test</u>. Well, if I had a blessed idea, it had better be my dream, so I started the mastermind on February 9, 2017 with a group of professional women, many of whom had written books and were coaches. This group gave me many ideas and suggestions for inspirational reading and led me to another training that I found on Facebook - "Life Visioning" with Michael Bernard Beckwith. I had been following him since seeing him on "The Secret." I watched his live stream of his trans-denominal church, Agape, and had gradually become more able to understand what he was saying. When I first listened to his audiobook in 2012, I thought, "This guy carries a lot of great energy. I can't understand half of what he says, but I like him." When I started the training in 2017, it finally started to click and I could make connections. The training with MBB was part of a larger platform called "Mindvalley." I had accidentally discovered a gold mine of training on everything from mindset, meditation, physical health, and developing intuition. I was on a mission.

I took more than five different classes in the two months between the time of the <u>Innerspace</u> book signing to the time I met with Tracey to tour the condo on April 8, 2017. I was in a completely different frame of mind by that time. I had met her with "How can I get a better process, so I can have some time off" mindset to a "What is it going to take to live my purpose" focus. While discussing the condo and what was happening in the real estate market, conversation turned to how I was doing physically. I told her I had been going to the chiropractor and while the back pain was better, the pain in my sternum was not. The chiropractor had shown me the pressure point where the pain originated from lack of forgiveness and suggested I try acupuncture. When I told Tracey, she asked, "Do you want it gone today?" I replied immediately, "Yes!"

After the Reiki session, I felt like a mass the size of a basketball was gone from my stomach. My thought in the moment was, "My life will never be the same!" How true! I started to think that I was a connector and a channeler. My meditations kept coming with the message to let go of control and that my purpose was to transform education. On April 27, 2017, I had my first acupuncture appointment and was told that people tend to make decisions faster after treatment because energy flow is cleared.

By May, I was pushing for a cruise to Europe, and my husband did not want to go on a cruise. We argued about it for a month until June, when he said he wanted to take a relocation from work. I was all in. I started a matrix of locations where his company had positions where he could apply. The top of my list was Spain. On June 13, 2017, I handed in resignations to every board, committee, and group where I was working or volunteering. I was ready to go! I started repairs on three of the properties we owned to prepare them for sale. The plan was to sell everything and go to Europe for at least two years. The messages I received in meditation and in readings were all focused on heart healing, physical healing, and forgiveness. When the relocation plans stalled, I started looking at where I could go to check out various locations in person and get him energized to go. I truly felt that taking a relocation would reset our lives and our marriage. I was growing quickly, and I wanted to get us all on the same path to growth and change.

From June through September, I spent most of my time in meditation, resting more and researching manifestation through intention. I made a trip to Walpole Island, Canada and did some genealogy research. I was searching for answers for my path from the past and from my present. I was searching everywhere I could think to search. Any messages I received, I followed.

During this time, I was drawn to the path of coaching and public speaking. I was not sure how to get started, so I started looking for people I knew who were already mentoring. I knew Karen Palka, with A Beautiful Me, who was mentoring 10-year-old girls on self-esteem in schools, and I asked her what it would take for me to work with them; I knew it would be a step on my path. In September, I had started working in the classrooms, which led me to Toastmasters to improve my speaking skills. At the first meeting. I was directed to the coach who was hosting the event and was already doing what I wanted to do. The next day I met her at an unrelated lunch, hired her, and started the business planning.

In October, I had another Reiki session. Tracey and I talked through the changes happening in my life. She told me that it was part of my path to heal people by seeing to the core of the issue and to the healing needed. In the next two weeks, I reconnected with a friend who had recently returned from Egypt, and I told her I was developing my coaching and public speaking skills to coach others to live their best lives. She put me in touch with her cousin who works in that field and lives in Lexington and Spain. By November 22, 2017, I was coaching with this lady, and on March 16, 2018, I was on a plane to the Canary Islands, Spain to teach at an experience retreat called "Remodel Your Habits, Remodel Your Life." This is where I was gifted my first orgonite from a shaman, Gregor Kocijancic.

It was the last day of the retreat, and I was leaving for home in the next day. When I held the orgonite, I could feel the electrical energy. I asked what it was; however, he was not there to explain. Others told me it was for putting by cell phones or Wi-Fi routers to keep the waves from bothering you while you sleep. I thought there must be more, but let it be and thought I would use it during my meditation since there was a large rose quartz crystal in the middle.

In April 2018, I started asking more questions because I could feel the electrical energy. Gregor started sending me information on the plates he makes to clean food and water. I wanted to test them, so I ordered a plate. I specifically asked for a plate to use for food, water, and meditation. At this point, I still was not 100 percent sure what this tool was, but I wanted it. When my coaching partner was on her way to the U.S. for a month-long visit and business meeting on April 28, 2018, she brought me four more of the hearts for my children and one plate. I started using the plate with avocados and tomatoes and noticed they were staying fresh longer. Then, I started experimenting with water and it tasted better. Then my daughter started using the plate for meditating, with great results. She also tried putting it under her bed and had the best sleep she had had in years. Given the results we were seeing, I wanted more information and to know the true power of orgonite. I used orgonite for over three months before I shared it with my energy healing groups.

On August 15, 2018, I had an urge to take the orgonite plate to The Wyld & The Wyrd store to share with the owner, Jen. She has been a Reiki Master since 1994 and promotes holistic healing. Once she touched it, she wanted one for herself. I was so excited to share this tool, and on August 21, 2018, I took it with me to the healing circle Tracey facilitates. I met Tracey early for coffee and as soon as she touched the large plate, she felt the energy and wanted one for herself. We then shared the plate with the circle, which led to three more plates being ordered. I worked back and forth with everyone who ordered to get their specific requests and intentions built into their individual tools. When the orders came in on September 12, 2018, I felt like I was flying down the road with all the Orgon energy in the car. I delivered the Canadian orders on September 14, 2018 to Tracey and others, each individually presented with their own instructions and intentions.

This is, by no means, the end of my story with Tracey. It is just the explanation of the beginning!

Cup Full Of Worthiness

When will I have the courage
to love myself and say,
"Enough is enough?"

By Laurie Smydo

It is 6:00 a.m. and I cannot sleep. I have taken the day off to spend the PD day with my children and to catch up on some much-needed relaxation and rest. But – I have let the actions of others ruin my day again! It is a common theme in my life lately. At the age of 42, you would think a grown woman would have mastered the art of caring for herself. I have learned though, since meeting Tracey, apparently, I am not the average woman. I am an empath and a healer, which is a lovely thing to think of oneself as, until you realize what it means and all it entails. I am in the midst of learning that as I give to everyone else, I, too, am also worthy of the same love, kindness, and empathy I give to others on a daily basis.

On January 1st of 2018, I opened myself up to the universe and told her I was ready to receive all my answers. I was ready to listen. I was ready to take action. Little did I know I would meet Tracey 26 days later and my entire world would change.

I believe the universe sent Tracey to me. I love psychic fairs and always go to them with friends. On that blessed day though, I decided I did not want a reading. I was just not feeling it. I was sad, in a rut in my life, and did not feel like listening to what I had already been told many times before. This was quite the contradiction of what I asked the universe to provide me with a few short weeks before. But when you ASK, and BELIEVE, guess what – you RECEIVE!

Tracey sat down at a table with my friend and me. I am not usually one for small talk or a conversation starter with strangers; however, this beautiful lady sat down at our table. She had just had a reading, and I was curious to know how it went. Half-way through our conversation, she looked at me with her kind eyes and asked to hold my hand. All she said to me was, "Honey, I know. I have been exactly where you are." Tears streamed down both our faces while my friend sat across the table with a shocked look of disbelief on her face. She, too, knew my struggles of late. I understand why this meeting of two souls took place this day. The universe sent Tracey to me because I am WORTHY!

It probably was only a day or two until I reached out to Tracey for a heart healing session. This first session of many with Tracey changed the course of my life. Tracey has a very special gift of understanding and knowing what is going on in your life, and then providing significant healing and guidance. She knew things about me, including my preponderance for existing for others and not living my life to my full potential. She was right. I had embraced my role as caregiver and leader throughout my entire life, whether it was planning an outing for friends, organizing social gatherings and events at work, leading projects, being there for people in times of crisis, and the list went on. It was all true and something I had prided myself on. But the real truth was I had been existing for others in my busy career, going through the motions of a being a wife, mother, boss, friend – there for everyone else, but rarely for myself. Don't get me wrong - I benefited a lot from these actions (beautiful friendships, great career opportunities, beautiful children), but at the end of the day, did I think I was worthy of all these things? Did I think I deserved them? Why did I deserve more?

Tracey told me I was existing instead of living. That was a huge 'ah ha' moment for me, one for which I will be forever grateful. She was 100 percent right. She lifted the veil off many issues that I constantly pushed aside. That day, she told me that I was worthy to have love and to receive those things in return that I had so freely given to others. You know what? I agreed with her. What the heck have I been doing? I am worthy. I AM SO WORTHY!!!

I have been to several sessions with Tracey since that day. She has become my guide, my mentor, and a very dear friend. She is my soul sister. Perhaps one of the biggest lessons she has taught me is how to move forward in life from the perspective of truth and kindness. I cannot even begin to describe how grateful I am for this lesson. She has taught me about acting from a place of love, instead of anger, sadness, duty, or guilt. Talk about turning negative feelings into positive acts of love and kindness! Just think about that for a moment. Instead of getting upset or annoyed by what someone has said or done to me or fearing how someone is going to react to what I need to say or a decision to be made, I instead flip these feelings to come from a place of acting in truth and kindness towards the other person. This action is very freeing and powerful.

When my heart comes forward from this perspective, I no longer feel scared or guilty. I am able to move forward with difficult discussions that I likely would have ignored or let go in the past because I was too afraid of the response, or just didn't want to deal with the negative outcome of the conversation. I did not want to make the conversation about my pain or my feelings. I have learned that when I come from a heartfelt perspective, I can use my gift of empathy to focus on the other person's challenges in the situation, while at the same time gaining back my power and freeing myself from the pain. I am moving forward from a perspective of truth, love, and kindness because I AM WORTHY.

What happens when I move forward in this manner? Boundaries are re-formed, and power is taken back. I no longer put up with the way I was treated in the past by ignoring, laughing or shrugging off something that deeply bothered me. That way of existing is no longer in alignment with how I want to live my life. I am a recovering conflict avoider and peacekeeper, so this has probably been one of the most challenging aspects of my life lesson. I certainly do not want to be perceived as a mean or demanding person, which is sometimes hard to do when you are in a leadership position. Awakened people are aware that repeating challenging situations and difficult lessons is truly a gift for us, to push us forward to our higher selves. If you choose to avoid it over and over again, a lesson will practically scream at you until you deal with it. I have heard the screams several times this year. But let me say this: over time, my reaction to things has calmed down significantly. Anger, frustration, and ego – all have quieted, and I can now attempt to come from a space of calm and observance when a challenging situation arises. I have much more patience, as well, when working through a problem and forming a solution, instead of rushing through a challenging situation to get away from the icky feelings that come along with it.

Am I perfect? Do I ever react in a way that is not in alignment with who I want to be? Absolutely, because I am a very passionate person and I am only human. Practice makes perfect – and that's what life is all about, right? I know I am worthy of practicing this until I get it right!

As I have had the pleasure of connecting with Tracey outside of our sessions, she has shared so many of her gifts with me. These gifts have helped develop so many areas of my life, including my passion for art. When I paint, I feel so free! Most creative people will get this. Whether you paint, write, or sing, it is almost as if you turn on autopilot and get lost during the time of creation. Something just takes over. I am truly not in control at all. I can have an opinion or stand back and look at a piece of art and know where it needs tweaking here and there. I have been told many times that people see guides, spirits, or angels in my paintings. I have painted only a few pieces with angels in them (which you may have seen in Tracey's healing room). Most of my paintings are large, abstract pieces, where people pick their colours and size and then off I go and do my thing. I always sage and ask Spirit for guidance before every painting session. Perhaps this is where Spirit is showing it is with me in the process! Sometimes Tracey will text me and tell me I need to get in the studio. When she tells me that, you better believe I am running down to my studio if I can in that very moment!

One morning, I was feeling full of gratitude for having met Tracey, and I decided to send her a quick message telling her how amazed and grateful I was for her coming into my life. She told me in return how much she needed that message that day. To even think I could brighten her day after all she has done for me is such an honour. She told me to go outside and plant my feet in the grass as she sent me a violet breath. I can tell you this – when you are in your forties, you really give up worrying what your neighbors might think of your standing barefoot on your lawn in your pajamas, drinking in the sunlight and taking deep breaths, raising arms to the sky. The second I closed my eyes, I saw the most beautiful violet light. I ran back inside to tell Tracey what I had seen and painted a small watercolor casually while we were on the phone. To see this painting, please visit my Instagram page at las_artstudio and check out this sweet, tiny watercolor entitled VIOLET BREATH.

After we hung up the phone, I sent this image to Tracey. Of course, she immediately saw a larger figure releasing violet breath into a figure below. I did not paint this on purpose. I was simply trying to recreate the shades of violet I saw when I closed my eyes. I am starting to learn to accept that some of my paintings are divinely guided. I am trying to be open to this gift and plan to spend the next year cultivating this tool to be able to share this gift with others. My intention is to help people draw in their own spirit, angels, and guides. With Tracey's help, I know I will be able to develop this further and share this light with people who need it, who want to share their light with others, and want to be light bearers themselves.

I believe Tracey encouraged me to write this chapter because I am a normal person who has experienced various levels of healing this year. I have a regular job. I am a creative being who loves to paint. I am a mother, a sister, a friend, a girl who likes to have a glass of wine with my girlfriends on a Friday night. I am just like you. I, like Tracey, am aware that many are being called to share their light and experiences in the world right now. People are waking up!

I have experienced beauty and joy this year in the face of pain. I have done the work. I asked the universe for guidance and tried as graciously as possible to receive. I may not have liked all the answers, but the themes kept repeating until I could no longer stand it or had no choice other than to move forward.

Everyone has access to be open to these experiences in life. Read books, journal, get spiritual, meditate, be open to everything and anything, have a visit with Tracey. Do not ignore the messages and the people the Universe sends your way. There is meaning behind everything and everyone you meet. Do not ever second-guess if what you are seeing, hearing, believing, and feeling is real. IT IS! These messages and gifts we are seeing and hearing right now during this enlightened time are being sent to us all to help us align with our highest selves. It is happening because we are WORTH IT! As Tracey would say – how flucking cool is that?!?

Always in Love and Light,
Laurie

To see more of Laurie's artwork, you can follow her on Instagram or Facebook at LAS – Art Studio.

Cup Full Of Mystic

"A mystic is a person who seeks by contemplation and self-surrender to obtain unity with or absorption into the Deity of the Absolute, or who believes in the spiritual apprehension of truths that are beyond the intellect…Mysticism is the practice of religious ecstasies, together with whatever ideologies, ethics, rites, myths, legends, and magic may be related to them. It may also refer to the attainment of insight in ultimate or hidden truths, and to human transformation supported by various practices and experiences." Wikipedia.

Keegan is a mystic, self-proclaimed and also designated by other healing light workers. How did I know this before he even told me? You just need to spend no more than five minutes with this divine human being to know that being a Mystic is his all-encompassing truth. His company is called Keegan Spiritline. His email is keeganspiritline@gmail.com.

I met Keegan in spirit before I ever met him in body. That is a strange statement, but absolutely and completely accurate. I was introduced to his craft and collective skills and purchased his blessed wood bracelets and spell kits before I ever met him. He has a section of his own in the store, Gypsy Soul Trading Co., in our town. Keegan also represents himself at our local farmers' market, which is where I met him face to face in the summer of 2018.

As I walked up to Keegan, I felt the spiritual presence within him. I will do my very best to share my experience of our connection when The Divine introduced us to each other. We locked eyes and were immediately transfixed, entwined, united in each other's soul space and energy. We hugged and embraced like long-lost friends from another entire galaxy. He said so many personal things to me that day that resonated so deeply I can still hear his words; but more than the words, the truth of them healed layers upon layers of my heart. I was instantly validated for being an ambassador for The Divine through Keegan's messages of purity and honesty, as thick, loving energy left his body and wrapped around me like a huge blanket of love. He could see and feel parts of my soul that I had not validated in a very long time, if ever. His honesty, depth, truth, and love were like God himself was speaking through Keegan. I was face to face with the presence of The Divine through this mystic connection.

We held each other for some time, exchanging messages of love and hope, allowing each other to feel. This feeling left me in a state of absorbing the purest form of love to an extent I had not experienced before. After we connected, I knew I would somehow forever stay connected to this loving energy soul person. I knew my life in some ways would forever change by our meeting. To say I am in love with Keegan would be an understatement. I need him in a way I know is healthy and non-compromising for both of us. This love goes beyond our normal experience of love; it is free and honest and committed. We work together for the greater cause.

After we stopped exchanging, I asked him to pick a bracelet for my sister-in-law who had lost one of her sons at a very young age. I wanted to give it to her the next time we were together. As he was looking for a bracelet, I went into Gypsy Soul and grabbed my book and music CD and signed a copy for him. When I came back out of the store, we handed each other the gifts we had selected for each other and exchanged equally. I then invited Keegan to the next circle healing session. Keegan brought gifts that night and selflessly shared them after the teaching that evening. He went around to everyone in circle, giving them a personal message of divine love, wisdom, and hope. We were all in love from that point on.

I spoke with Keegan about coming to do a teaching of his own at circle. That night as he was presenting, The Divine whispered on my heart, "His Keegan, our Keegan, is a Mystic." The word suits him; he represents the meaning of this word in every way. When I introduced Keegan that night before his teaching, I introduced him as a Mystic, which he immediately claimed as true. He captured our hearts and our souls and educated us on the beautiful essence and life of Canadian-mined Amethyst. He taught us that night Amethyst has living energy, and he taught us how to care for our crystal child. He gave each of us permission to select our very own crystal child. He continued his evening of healing, going around the circle and with his own breath he blew spirit life into our new crystal babies as we held them in our hands. He channeled his sacred guide, a phoenix, who then channeled messages for us individually, straight from The Divine. I cried rivers of healing tears, releasing toxins of low self-worth, when I received my message. I still hear the words from him that resonate truth and love for me from The Divine. We were all healed and elevated to a transitioned state of grace and love that evening.

I have invited our Keegan to share in his own way and with his own words how it feels to represent a body with mystic gifts in this age and time and how he uses those gifts to channel, teach, heal, and advise. Please welcome and enjoy Keegan as much as I cherish this gifted, wise, human, spirit-led being.

In Keegan's words:

I see you through the eyes of The Divine. I see you through the fragments of what exists around us. I live in a world where I am here, and yet not here. I am a Mystic. I am human, yet living as a vessel to behold the natural, spiritual ecosystem that is on this earth. Even as I am writing this, I am receiving a message from the spirits that co-exist with me and my work on this earth, "They are all opening their eyes to the available medicine that The Divine has placed on this earth. They are readying themselves to heal what they felt could not be healed, and yet, here we are, and it is possible."

When I met Tracey, I knew that she was a part of The Divine, part of being, a living breathing effort of The Divine to heal, to inspire, to provide opportunity, to allow a state of medicine (pure healing of energy – mind, body, and soul) to be instilled in those who are looking for the golden touch on their person and their life. I am so honoured and grateful to take part in this medicine, the medicine woman who is Tracey and the divine well-spring that is her, that allows clear vision of self, clear vision of The Divine in a human embodiment on this earth. I am so happy to share of myself and to share my mysticism, to breach from my hermit living, thus allowing you to see a path that sees beyond this ever-living, expanding world.

I am a Mystic by varied trades. I have worked with several different spiritual modules, paradigms, mythos, tools, craft, and spiritual paraphernalia. I live within a spiritual movement from the time I wake up to the time I sleep. Even working within sleep, I receive knowledge beyond my open eyes looking at the physical world. I live with an altar space with statuary, candles, cauldron, crystals and crystal grid, and an assortment of tools like Tarot and Oracle decks and sacred objects connecting me to spirits, godheads, and energies within my work. I allow the voices and hands of the earth to have conjunctive access in sharing space within me, thus allowing an opening to all to be heard in their truth. I carry that truth with me in my day into the outside world, beyond this space I create between me and the expansive reality that we live in. I work with the spiritual archetypes that surround us and present their messages freely. Sometimes, I petition them for healing and services. There are other times I just form bonds with these energies because I feel their truth out, inviting their powerful truth and the worth it has for our world. We join in force with our combined energy, working, living side by side. I allow sacredness and energy to be a living choice – to allow it to be what it is: natural and freeing to the physical sensations and healing to the body, mind, and soul.

As Tracey indicated, I view this world with many an opportunity to meet its children. Mother Earth, Gaia, offers her children to us: the crystals, trees, plants, waterways, the ground on which we stand. We are all standing in this ecosystem that is connected, living full life in a way that we might not necessarily perceive. Have faith that all things in this world respond in kind, to you, your presence. I have gifted some of these children – these gemstones, because these are physical crystallizations of living parts of Mother Earth, each gem with its own identity and its own presence to hold. These crystals impart great knowledge and powerful, healing energy pulsating from within, reaching out to those who hold them, gifting the beholder touching upon their surface. I have also brought people into connection with Elementals that surround them and offer them guidance. I also assist in communicating with those entities who have lost their personal resonance and direction, with how they assist this world and the beings upon it.

I live in a state of reception, always ready to receive synergies of divine nature; to have the opportunity to experience a moment with spirits, energy, godheads, dimensional beings, others who see this world with open eyes and open hearts. I do not necessarily seek these occurrences; I merely play a part as an observer, a vessel, allowing these conjunctive energies access to the needed healing or messages that are imparted from these experiences. I often channel these messages or healing that is needed to take place in partnership with those who are a part of the surrounding spiritual/astral/dimensional ecosystem - the spirits of the land and of this earth who see us with divine eyes and understanding. This living energy has a wish for us to meet our potential, or more so, allow us to not fear that potential and allow it to be us – the unlimited, unopposed, soul that we are.

I live with a compassionate heart. I bring about the needed messages from me to you, from ancient energies that exist within this world and are a part of this world. I live in the lightness of what the ancient energies bring, the divine nature in everything. Healing is always possible and available to the people who meet me, the spiritual energies that meet me. I, myself, heal alongside this activity. I genuinely open the connection, a heartfelt connection, so that truth is revealed. The truth, then, has sight in all situations. This defines my work as a Mystic.

I seat myself before the ecstatic energy that surrounds all, and I say into this energy, "Where or with whom do I meet?" The system of spiritual energy, of divine nature, of dimensional creation, then begins to hum and sing. I then see from the ground up the world come alive in its truth, the same truth that exists within us, the same truth that teaches us the awareness that we have always been. I see the spirits of the land wake up. They flex and stretch, from the smallest pixie to the greatest serpentine spirit lying in the forest, announcing its presence and allowing the voice of the land to be heard. I see the air fill with faces ecstatically smiling from winds of change. I see animal spirits leaping and running endlessly through the forests and above the ground that no longer limits them. I see the sky fill with the spirits of lights, rainbow colours, winged spirits singing hymns and giving joyous praises upon Mother Earth so that all partake of the energy and heal. I see it all! I see the faces that hide in neighbourhood gardens. I see spirits that have forgotten themselves and haunt streets and buildings, feeling their need to come back to remembering their nature of Source, reconnecting, loving, divine. I see this all and I know that it has all been here before and will always remain. Being a Mystic, you come to understand that all knowledge of what we imagine or once thought to be here has always been and it will never change. You come to accept the natural mythos, never-ending quests, the magic, that folklore was not just a tool to teach, but to garnish the fact that our living is always beside these spiritual paradigms, spiritual shifts, living and breathing beside us in a very natural way.

Of course, you would, or could, probably ask, "This all sounds amazing, but where do you find the time to see this? How are you seeing this?" Well, dear soul reading this, I spend my waking hours in kinship and connection with all of this – there is no separation of this living for me. I am a committed connection to all living. I see with open eyes, open soul, open mind, open heart.

You might think that this is an existence where you could feel separation from others, but there is no separation, no extra cost for this living. Instead, there is vibrancy and deep understanding to be honoured and show gratitude for, because when I meet others, I am humbled not only by the sight of meeting another face to face, but I get to be witness to another, to see growth in another, to see The Divine and the healing that is taking place in another – and so I heal. I receive messages, and I get to express and console those innermost parts of myself, as well, for when I meet another in healing as the conduit of delivering a message, I receive all the same in return – I channel and I get to experience that healing, that energy, that union that comes from the centre of ourselves and reaches out to the assistance of that divine, ecstatic energy. Every living, breathing moment with another, no matter how long or short it is, is a connection to an expression of The Divine, Source, God, Gods, Goddesses, the cosmos.

I meet with all these energies when I channel, when I draw cards, (Tarot and Oracle), to give voice and colour for the spiritual representation of the energy present. This is done by instilling myself as the conduit channel for energy needed in the deliverance of the healing message. I look at the image, the sensation that is being guided to me, from me, from something other than me, and I become the voice for this energy. I allow it to bring resolution and its personal message to the day, or to the client with whom I am working. I quiet myself. In conjunction with energy upon me, I give this living energy permission to counsel and teach through me – I channel and I experience at the same time. I allow the presence, the motion, the being, the energy to be gratified and honoured for its worthiness in its healing and its moment to reach out to those who need its assistance. I give these spirits, godheads, divine facets, natural spiritual occurrences, space to be – space apart from me, and yet, through me it exists. Committed as one force, connected with these beings, these energies, we exist. Working together, we become a part of the integrated healing taking place the world over.

As I have grown in my spirituality, my mysticism, my soul worthiness, and my understanding of self, where I have come from and where I have been (living on this planet, many incarnations, many lessons beyond this sphere that is Earth), I have found my truth through my perception of life that the soul, the soul within humans, is everlasting. Living as human beings, my experience has taught me that being human, we tend to separate spiritual movements, spiritual paradigms, and then place limits to what can and cannot be.

Now, of course as a standard, we eventually come to know through life lessons there are limits to the 3D/4D living. One might entertain the notion beyond our world that there are interactive parts of life existing in our universal dimensions. We might even suggest this existence would never want to have anything to do with us, to engage, to share anything, to equate, to help us possibly grow, affecting our living, heightening our own personal qualities. I can assure you there are—or more so, I can offer that there is—something at the ready to bring healing in any way it can, as it is always willing – those facets of The Divine. These living gemstones of this earth, the trees and their representing spirits, the Fae and

Elementals of the earth, the angelic, the gods and godheads of many past civilizations, the ancestors to your blood, the cosmic representations and the bodies they form – these are all at the ready and have connections to us from the divine creation we were made from. There is medicine in this divine nature – there is the tincture, the cure in divine nature, whether it is from the facets of The Divine or The Divine itself with its open hands to you, showering you in its light, its love, washing away the disease that concerns you, that halts your understanding, your progression in life.

I am a Mystic by living, by experience, by love and nature, and so I am offering this to you and because, again, I am receiving messages as I am writing this for lovely Tracey, this gift for you reading this, that there is so much more for you – not to endure, not to suffer, but so much more at hand that will allow you to reach and see your soul worthiness – to say yes to your unlimited self.

Know that just as there is value, connection, and honest-to-goodness healing within nature, the reality that surrounds you, this connection in its totality is always a part of you. There is no disconnect – just as I stated for myself, this living has no disconnect for me, and so it is the same for you. And so, just as I am the Mystic who seats himself before The Divine and the spiritual occurrences that exist around us, you are living in that same space, as well. All you need to do is open your heart, be aware of the self, and speak to The Divine within you. He will respond with love and openness to you.

Right now, as I am typing away, I see one of my favorite animals appearing, representing himself within my sight, with my eyes and heart open to the moment. I see a pure white baby fox, its energy beaming with joy – a representation of this book and of the people it touches – to be able to receive this healing openly, to walk into the hedges of nature and come back out with a greater healing instilled. This message, if accepted within, is adaptive healing that is starting anew within you - a healing of something more that may have been missing, that last drop of ever-clear water quenching thirst so you may not waver in your search for more.

All that I collectively acquire in my living as Keegan, a dedicated Mystic, I choose always to bring that direct connection, combined with Source. I will bring resolution to others that there is no disconnect in all that we feel from our heart. I promise to channel pure, honest kindness and truth in this world and its spiritual reality, associating, interacting, sharing with anyone who is seeking. I hope to see more people come to the temple of their worth and be nourished in its light, its radiance, its space; to know that we are all sacred vessels, we are all attuned to this "spiritual stuff," and that when you ask it for help, for healing, that you don't shy away from your worthiness of receiving that healing; that you embrace it; that you bask in it.

I am Keegan. I am a Mystic. I see this world and sit myself in its endlessness, its nexus of colour and light, teamed with its ever-present, entranced beings, and I smile on my heart. I smile because I see that, no matter the case, this world is without end. Despite the fact that Mother Nature may end, as she does exist as a living being, in truth this world itself will never cease. The Divine and its flow of source that we gain from our earth in our living world is the experience of the soul/body creations. I am delighted to be a vessel for this sharing, providing a channel of the knowing that everything is relevant to rebuilding star bodies, bearing witness to these vessels, these beacons of loving energy that are unique to behold, and witnessing the growth of their own specific realities. I, Keegan, will maintain this commitment to Source and myself to be on guard, to lovingly provide anything and everything The Divine sends my way. I will remain open and on guard so that my awareness remains constant and keen. I will love entirely and guide anyone seeking truth.

Cup Full Of Heart To Heart

You would think, I suppose, if you are a person like me who is over-analytical and has been questioning the better part of my life, that I would have things all figured out; that the positive energy I invite into my heart, my first thought, my main focus when I open my eyes in the morning, would override the grey skies and cold rain. You would think that, maybe, I might have a few answers, or at least have some solutions as to how we can, in community, come together, understanding and accepting all the wrongs of our world. I preach a mean story of light versus darkness. I work hard every day choosing to commit to spreading positive energy for the sake of the broken; inviting white light energy to spread internally in my own life, aiding in the discovery of my own self-worth.

Truth is truth, and it does not make life even one bit easier knowing it and then trying your hardest to live in the light of it. In fact, sometimes it is almost impossible to stay in the moment. The power of the moment holds us physically here, hearts beating, feeling, knowing the truth in things you choose to accept or disregard. We accept the truth and forge on to spread this internal light, this gift of love, where at times, believe it or not, it may not be accepted or even wanted, let alone respected.

I am a firm believer that when you make a commitment, you grow in it and through it. Commitment changes you. It becomes who you are, your focus, positive energy, and it settles in on you. You grow in this way of becoming, this choice you made. Personally, the choices I made over thirty years ago taught me some valuable and very painful lessons. Would I choose them again if my future was revealed? Not likely! I think I would have had more faith in myself and sacrificed differently. I can only say now that the knowledge I gained through learning my lessons taught me to walk taller, growing in grace on my path. So, how could I have made that kind of conscientious decision without experiencing the lessons?

This brings me right back around, full circle. I have been cocooning this past week while writing, and since I don't allow myself this quiet downtime, or what some people would think is non-productive, it feels strangely foreign. We are programmed our entire human life to be productive, or, to further this thought, we tend to feel we are simply not pulling our weight in society, home, work, or responsibilities if we take some time for ourselves. We are made to feel the 'important things' we do with the time given to us are the most productive way to be. Setting examples of productivity gains favour or love in and for the people to whom we are most connected, and, of even higher importance, with the strangers seeking unconditional invitations of love and acceptance.

Those new beings who are drawn to you seeking love and light are sometimes more important than the secure connections with whom you have cemented foundations. Those new souls are drawn to your beacon of light, and, if you are in awareness, you will recognize the hunger and need to belong. This may be because they have a life full of loneliness, abuse, or addictions they do not have the strength to address, let alone overcome. A kind word, a friendly gesture, a heart smile, a listening ear to lost and lonely people searching for something they may feel pulled or drawn to, but cannot quite identify – all are so needed and so worthwhile!

It is interesting that as I write this in my beautiful, safe space, I am reminded how my day started. As often happens in the Canadian winter, the cold, damp, blustery weather was threatening to break my door. As the darkness of the overcast day started to seep into the window, sneaking in between the open blinds, I started to remember those same triggers I have received this time of the year for the past several years. Why should I let my guilt or vulnerability or self-doubt from the past and the power they have over the way I feel or think get in the way of my present? These dark thoughts steal from me God-given moments of life, changing my internal beauty and the energy of my day. I have enough to think about without taking on the memories of experiences that preceded the lessons represented in those triggers. So, I let them go and I let my negativity go. I stopped thinking about how guilty I was feeling and started thinking about how I am grateful and how full my life is.

I got up and looked out the window and saw the sunshine peeking through the dark day, literally like a sign, and then, in an instant, I stopped feeling overwhelmed and started feeling like the channel God intended me to be. In that magical, miracle, moment of love, I saw the connection, felt the empowered growth, and knew I was not alone in my fight. Then an angel texted me and said, "We would love to do dinner tonight. We miss you and would love to spend time with you." And just like that, the power of attraction deepens and fills my cup full of magic.

I showered with this positive awareness growing in me. With this kind of power, I knew the day was just going to turn somehow. And so it did! It truly did! I took extra care in doing my hair pretty for Joe - he likes it when I have spent time on my hair; it makes him feel proud of me, I guess, and he thinks good thoughts that make him want to smile. I carried on and after getting lunch for my sweetie, I packed up my laptop and made a conscious decision to go to the local library to work, along with the master writers filling the shelves.

Still reflecting from my morning, I felt empowered. My body was alive with new found respect for hard core authors, information, wisdom. Along my walk to get to the library, I ran into a few more good-hearted people and my smile deepened. My mission of reflection grew bigger in the awareness developing in the day and the learning it would bring me. I was savoring and gathering these collective, powerful interactions while heading to my intended destination. I needed this exchange and to receive loving, prana energy to start working, manifesting my writing, combined with a need to share with you. I started this chapter not quite sure of the intentions or the direction this chapter was heading, except a deep knowing it was meant to be about a cup full of gratitude.

I have not had a library card for years, but on this day, I signed up and officially became a member of the Strathroy Middlesex Library. The last time I even remember signing up for a library card was when I was around the age of eleven. I had a slight flashback, remembering the coveted experience of feeling, belonging, to a club of special people. Still smiling, I got settled on a laptop desk, but for some reason I could not find a power source at that station, so I moved my computer to another spot. In this spot, I could see more people. There was an elderly man sitting by the window, quietly reading a book.

I became absorbed in my writing. Then suddenly, surprising myself, I felt my heart tug - not a huge tug; just a quiet, gentle tug. I looked up and turned my head towards the man, and he smiled. The smile was from his soul, and I noticed that his appearance was old, worn, soiled, but what I really saw in that moment was his internal beauty. I had just purchased a bracelet from Gypsy Soul, knowing when I purchased the bracelet that I would be giving it away. I stopped typing, got up, walked over and stuck my hand out. The startled man looked confused. He asked me to wait as he put in his hearing aid. He reached into the pocket of his stained, worn coat, producing a hearing aid, old-fashioned but functional. I waited for him to adjust it and turn it on. I stuck my hand out again and said, "My name is Tracey." He said, "My name is Pat." I asked if I could sit down, and he said I could. We had a small conversation and he asked me what I was typing. I told him I was writing a book. He did not seem to understand this answer, so I went on to say I had just purchased a healing bracelet and I wanted to gift him with it. I put it on his wrist and he registered shock again, but this time with a look of sheer child-like pleasure, melting my heart. I told him he needed the bracelet and it would help him to feel special and to find peace and joy. I went back to writing, and he went back to reading a true story about a Canadian serial killer. Interesting, his choice of reading, but the truth is we are all drawn to both dark and light energy and everyone has a story to tell.

Not once did I feel anything but joy in those few spun gold moments. The chain of events following will gift me forever. Pat stepped out for a few minutes, and when he returned, he came up to me and very shyly, very gently, asked for my autograph. Wow! My autograph! Seriously, that was the very last thing I ever expected. God lives in every single one of us, in all forms, all walks, all beings… Sometimes we just need to break out of our routine, our personal, safe comfort zone, to notice our own shackles and blinders, bringing new vision so we see with new eyes Divine presence face to face.

As I was still digesting the interaction, a nice, young man in a wheelchair approached me quietly, softly asking for assistance. It was obvious he needed help and was trying to pull himself up in his chair. He directed me, and I became his hands as we worked together, him stating his needs, me complying with his direction and requests. He let out a big sigh and looked directly into my eyes, saying with dignity, "Thank you, Madam." He then proceeded to wheel himself away, leaving me awestruck while he was oblivious to anyone else watching. He had a purpose-driven mission of his own.

As I reflect, I feel how my day turned out differently, inspired from heartfelt awareness, in having this experience of our little town library. We have a free sanctuary, full of wisdom, love, warmth, for special people seeking a safe, non-judgmental place to feel communion. Moments like this are new, reflective landmarks that layer my cup, encouraging, educating, teaching me a knowing that is imperative for our survival. As we continue living as divine loving energy, we learn to pay all things forward if we are going to stay strongly committed to the good in all of us. If you chose to look past your own needs and desires and straight into the face of someone with whom you can share goodness, I promise you one thing from the bottom of my soul. When you look, you will see the reflection of your own soul shining back at you! It is your own truth, a reflection you will recognize, that we, no matter what, are all connected to one grand source, entwined, united in love.

I am not sure if I can even begin to fully understand all my life lessons, but today, my action of love reveals truth, encompassing awareness, helping me grow in so many ways. I hope that I can still reach out for all who are called to me. I hope that I can always stay humbled in the changes and the growing. I hope that I will, in all ways, never, ever be too busy to recognize divine love and light in all people, places, and personal and painful experiences.

This life, my life, is moistened by rich tears of my own mixing with real tears of people healing in my arms, in my face, on my shoulder, sharing heart to heart, soul to soul. Some days, this heavy healing has the temporary effect of splitting my body and soul in a crippling state. This is temporary and sincerely awesome! I choose this work and it chooses me. It is my life's purpose, and this purpose keeps me wisely humbled, adding layers upon layers of experience, secured, deeply seated in the middle of the core of my entire being. How very special these moments are, as I gather them as treasures, securing my place in this life and the people who happen to walk into my days, my nights, my world.

You can choose this life, too, without giving up your Chicago popcorn and funny twisted movies. You can have your glass of rich red wine or your cocktail or your coffee, tea, hot chocolate. You can dedicate time to a person who is mute and tell them all the wonders and gifts you see in them. Or you can take the biggest roller coaster ride of your life at the biggest water park you ever imagined. You can have everything without giving up anything by choosing to stay in all that life presents to you, embracing all life's treasures with open arms and an open heart.

I happen to believe we are all worth it. I believe in every single person on this planet. I believe you all make a difference. Why? It is simple, yet most profound: it is because you were born! It is your destiny. You are gifted life again and again to discover, searching then discovering your purpose, without judgment. Eventually, you will find it. Eventually, you will become all you initially set out to be, experiencing all the lessons you set out to learn. Sit back and relax if you can. The ride is amazing, intense, magical, painful, and worth every single moment you get to live in this amazing gift of life!

My wish is that every single one of you reading this book embraces wholeness, gathering all you need to fill your cup. My wish is that every person finds their birthright, their own internal, anointed, and personally designated healer within the core of their own internal, and external, self. My wish is that peace reigns internally, building hope, drawing from a love within so strong that it allows you all to recapture and hone the whole person you were born to be. Love is the only reality we have. Spread it, share it, become the essence of it!

Love you all eternally! May light fill all the tiny holes in your being, bringing you to a place of wholeness.

Love and light.
Forever yours,

Tracey L. Pagana